I0019962

C++ PROGRAMMING: LEARN TO CODE FROM SCRATCH

A Step-by-Step Guide to Object-Oriented Programming in C++

THOMPSON CARTER

All rights reserved

No part of this book may be reproduced, distributed, or transmitted in any form or by any means without the prior written permission of the publisher, except in the case of brief quotations embodied in critical reviews and certain other noncommercial uses permitted by copyright law.

TABLE OF CONTENTS

CHAPTER 21: NETWORKING IN JAVA

INTRODUCTION

Welcome to *C++ Programming: Learn to Code from Scratch*. This book is designed to guide you step-by-step through the essentials of C++ programming, from the very basics of writing your first program to tackling advanced topics such as data structures, object-oriented programming, and even building a complete application from scratch. Whether you are new to programming or coming to C++ from another language, this book will walk you through everything you need to know in a clear and practical way.

Why Learn C++?

C++ is one of the most popular and widely used programming languages in the world. It has powered everything from simple applications to complex, large-scale systems that handle high-performance computing, graphics, video games, and even embedded systems found in cars and smart devices. Despite being created decades ago, C++ continues to evolve, remaining a highly relevant language for many applications today. The skills you gain from learning C++ will open doors to diverse fields, and understanding its concepts can make it easier to learn other languages.

Here are some key reasons why C++ remains an essential language to learn:

1. **Performance and Control**: C++ is known for its efficiency and control over system resources, making it ideal for

applications that require high performance, such as gaming engines, operating systems, and real-time computing.

2. **Versatility**: C++ is a general-purpose language that can be used across different domains, whether you are developing desktop applications, mobile apps, or even software for embedded systems.

3. **Foundation for Other Languages**: Learning C++ builds a strong foundation for understanding other programming languages like Java, C#, and even Python. Its syntax and programming concepts serve as a bridge to other languages, making it easier to learn and adapt to new technologies.

4. **Job Opportunities**: Many tech companies, particularly in industries like gaming, finance, and engineering, rely on C++ for critical applications. This means that C++ developers are consistently in demand.

What to Expect from This Book

This book takes a practical, hands-on approach to teaching C++. Instead of focusing heavily on theory or dense computer science concepts, we'll jump straight into writing code, solving problems, and creating small projects to cement what you learn. Here's a general roadmap of what you can expect as you progress through the book:

1. **Starting with the Basics**: We begin with an introduction to programming concepts and setting up your environment.

You'll write your first "Hello, World!" program, learn about variables, data types, and operators, and gain an understanding of control structures like loops and conditions.

2. **Building a Strong Foundation**: Once you've mastered the fundamentals, we dive deeper into topics like functions, arrays, and pointers. These are essential tools for any C++ programmer, allowing you to create flexible, reusable code.

3. **Advanced Concepts and Data Structures**: C++ offers robust data handling capabilities. You'll learn about structures, strings, and work with complex data structures like linked lists, stacks, and queues. Understanding these will make you a more versatile and effective programmer.

4. **Object-Oriented Programming**: One of the hallmarks of C++ is its support for object-oriented programming (OOP). You'll learn about classes, inheritance, polymorphism, and other core OOP principles that make your code more organized, modular, and easier to maintain.

5. **Memory Management and Concurrency**: These more advanced topics include pointers, memory management, and multithreading. We'll cover how to handle memory effectively to avoid memory leaks and manage concurrency with multiple threads to make your programs faster and more efficient.

6. **Practical Application Development**: To conclude, you'll bring together everything you've learned by building a

console-based application from scratch—a Personal Finance Manager. This project integrates multiple concepts and demonstrates how C++ can be used to create meaningful, real-world applications.

Who Is This Book For?

This book is written for anyone who wants to learn C++ programming from scratch. No prior programming experience is necessary, although some familiarity with general computer usage will help. Each chapter builds upon the previous one, so you can follow the book from start to finish and gradually deepen your knowledge.

If you have some programming experience, you'll still find value here. The book's in-depth explanations and real-world examples cover everything from beginner to advanced topics, allowing you to strengthen your understanding or fill in any gaps in your knowledge.

How to Use This Book

- **Follow Along with Examples**: Each concept is accompanied by clear code examples. I encourage you to type out the code yourself rather than just reading it. Typing the code allows you to better internalize the syntax and get comfortable with C++.
- **Practice Exercises**: At the end of most chapters, you'll find practice exercises. These are designed to reinforce what

you've learned and give you hands-on experience. If you get stuck, don't be discouraged! Problem-solving is a core part of programming, and each challenge will help deepen your understanding.

- **Project-Based Learning**: Throughout the book, we'll build small projects, which culminate in a complete console-based application. These projects allow you to apply what you've learned in a real-world setting and provide you with practical, portfolio-ready examples of your coding skills.

Learning C++ in the Real World

C++ has a reputation for being a bit challenging to learn due to its depth and complexity. This book aims to make learning C++ as approachable as possible by using plain language, real-world examples, and practical exercises. You'll find that each chapter builds naturally on the last, gradually introducing new concepts without overwhelming you.

It's important to remember that learning to program is like learning a new language; it takes practice, patience, and persistence. Along the way, you may encounter bugs, syntax errors, or parts of the language that seem confusing at first. This is entirely normal. Every programmer goes through it, and every challenge you overcome will make you a stronger coder.

Key Concepts You'll Learn

Here's a brief overview of some of the key concepts you'll master:

1. **Data Types and Variables**: Understanding the types of data C++ works with and how to store and manage it.

2. **Control Structures**: Mastering loops, if-else statements, and switch cases for making decisions within your programs.

3. **Functions and Modularity**: Breaking down code into reusable pieces to simplify complex tasks.

4. **Pointers and Memory Management**: Working with pointers to manage memory efficiently, a core concept unique to C++ and critical for performance.

5. **Object-Oriented Programming**: Learning how to model real-world problems by creating classes and objects, the foundation of many modern programming paradigms.

6. **Data Structures**: Exploring arrays, linked lists, stacks, queues, and other structures that make it easier to organize and manipulate data.

7. **File Handling**: Making data persistent by reading from and writing to files.

8. **Templates and the STL**: Using generic programming techniques and the Standard Template Library to build flexible, reusable code.

9. **Multithreading and Concurrency**: Leveraging the power of modern processors by running multiple tasks in parallel.

By the end of this book, you'll have a solid understanding of these topics and be well-equipped to continue learning C++ on your own or even tackle another programming language with confidence.

Why This Book Is Unique

This book emphasizes practical, example-based learning. Here's how it stands out:

- **Real-World Applications**: Instead of abstract examples, you'll find exercises and projects that reflect real-life applications, making the learning experience more engaging.
- **Project-Based Approach**: Each concept leads naturally into the next, culminating in a hands-on project that integrates everything you've learned.
- **Clear Explanations**: Concepts are explained in plain language, without unnecessary jargon, making the material accessible to beginners and approachable for all readers.

What's Next?

Learning C++ will give you the tools to build software for nearly any platform, from desktop applications to embedded systems. Once you complete this book, you'll be ready to move on to specialized areas of C++—whether it's advanced system programming, game development, or even graphical applications. Many of the skills you learn in C++ will transfer to other languages and areas of programming, from understanding basic programming logic to working with complex algorithms.

Staying Motivated and Moving Forward

Programming is an incredibly rewarding skill, and with each chapter, you'll see yourself building stronger skills and gaining confidence. As you work through the book, remember to take breaks, seek help if you need it, and revisit concepts that seem challenging. Learning to code can sometimes feel like solving a complex puzzle, but with every problem solved, you'll build valuable skills that will serve you in both personal projects and professional endeavors.

I hope that by the end of this book, you'll not only have a solid understanding of C++ but also the confidence and excitement to keep learning, experimenting, and building. Let's get started on this journey to mastering C++—and enjoy the process of transforming ideas into code that you can share with the world.

CHAPTER 1: INTRODUCTION TO C++ AND PROGRAMMING BASICS

Objective

This chapter introduces C++ as a powerful programming language and lays the groundwork for understanding programming fundamentals. By the end, readers will know how to set up a C++ development environment and write a simple "Hello, World!" program.

What is C++?

C++ is a versatile, high-performance programming language created by Bjarne Stroustrup in the early 1980s as an extension of the C programming language. Known for its speed and efficiency, C++ allows developers to write code that's closer to the machine level than higher-level languages, making it ideal for tasks requiring direct hardware control and high efficiency, like systems programming, embedded systems, and game development.

C++ is widely used in fields such as:

- **Game Development**: Used in developing major game engines like Unreal Engine.
- **Operating Systems**: A significant portion of Windows, macOS, and Linux contains C++.

- **Software Applications**: Adobe applications, such as Photoshop, are C++ powered.
- **Real-Time Systems**: Embedded systems, robotics, and other real-time control systems rely heavily on C++.

Why Learn C++?

Learning C++ gives you a strong foundation in programming due to its control over hardware, comprehensive standard library, and fundamental concepts like object-oriented programming (OOP). Many modern languages (like Java, C#, and Python) borrow C++ syntax and concepts, so mastering it can make learning these languages easier.

Setting Up a Development Environment

To begin coding in C++, we need two primary tools: a compiler and a text editor or an integrated development environment (IDE).

1. **Choosing a Compiler**
   - A compiler translates C++ code into machine-readable instructions. Popular options include:
     - **GCC (GNU Compiler Collection)**: Available on Linux, macOS, and Windows (via MinGW).
     - **Clang**: Known for its fast compile times and error diagnostics.

- **MSVC (Microsoft Visual C++)**: Available with Visual Studio on Windows.

2. **Choosing an IDE or Text Editor**

   o IDEs offer a one-stop workspace with text editing, debugging, and compiling features. Recommended IDEs for beginners include:

      - **Visual Studio** (Windows)
      - **Code::Blocks** (Cross-platform)
      - **CLion** (Cross-platform by JetBrains, requires a paid license after the trial)
      - **Visual Studio Code** (Cross-platform with C++ extensions)

3. **Installing and Setting Up**

   o **Windows**: Install Visual Studio or MinGW to get GCC. Once installed, configure the PATH environment variable so you can run C++ commands from the command line.

   o **MacOS**: Install Xcode (which includes Clang) or use homebrew to install GCC.

   o **Linux**: Most distributions come with GCC pre-installed, but if not, use the package manager (e.g., sudo apt install gcc on Ubuntu) to install it.

Writing Your First C++ Program: "Hello, World!"

Now that we've set up the environment, let's dive into writing the classic "Hello, World!" program. This program is a traditional first step in programming that outputs a simple message to the screen. Let's break down the steps and syntax involved.

1. **Creating a New File**
   - Open your IDE or text editor.
   - Create a new file and save it as hello.cpp. C++ source files have the .cpp extension.

2. **Understanding the Code Structure**

   Here's the code for our "Hello, World!" program:

   cpp

```cpp
#include <iostream>
using namespace std;

int main() {
    cout << "Hello, World!" << endl;
    return 0;
}
```

3. **Code Breakdown**
   - **#include <iostream>**: This line includes the standard input-output library. iostream stands for

"input-output stream," which enables us to use cout (for output) and cin (for input).

- o **using namespace std;**: The std namespace contains all the standard C++ library names. By adding this line, we avoid having to prefix standard functions with std::. For beginners, this helps simplify code, but as you progress, it's best to explicitly use std:: for clarity.

- o **int main()**: This is the entry point of every C++ program. The main function is where execution starts.

- o **cout << "Hello, World!" << endl;**: cout is used for output, directing data to the console. The << operator sends data to cout, and endl represents a newline, moving the cursor to the next line.

- o **return 0;**: This statement indicates that the program has ended successfully. It's a convention to return zero if everything worked as expected.

4. **Compiling and Running the Program**

To run this program, we first need to compile it. Here's how to do that based on the tools you might be using:

- o **Using Command Line** (for GCC/MinGW):
    - ▪ Open your terminal or command prompt.
    - ▪ Navigate to the directory where hello.cpp is saved.

- Run: g++ hello.cpp -o hello
- This command compiles hello.cpp into an executable file named hello.
- Now, run the executable: ./hello (Linux/macOS) or hello (Windows).

  o **Using Visual Studio Code or IDEs**:
    - If you're using Visual Studio Code, press F5 to compile and run the program.
    - For other IDEs like Code::Blocks or Visual Studio, select the "Run" or "Build and Run" option.

5. **Expected Output** When executed, the output should look like this:

Hello, World!

Programming Basics in C++

With the setup and first program in place, let's discuss the essentials that underpin all C++ programs.

1. **Basic Syntax**
   o C++ is case-sensitive, so Main and main would be different identifiers.
   o Every C++ statement ends with a semicolon (;).
   o Blocks of code are defined with curly braces {}.

2. **Comments**

- o Comments are non-executable parts of the code that help document it for readability.
- o Single-line comment: // This is a comment
- o Multi-line comment: /* This is a multi-line comment */

3. **Data Types and Variables**

- o **Data Types** define the type of data a variable can hold, like integers, floating-point numbers, characters, etc.
- o **Variables** are named storage locations in memory to hold data values.
- o Common types include:
    - ▪ int: Holds integer values (e.g., 10, -3).
    - ▪ float/double: Holds decimal numbers.
    - ▪ char: Holds a single character (e.g., 'A').
    - ▪ bool: Holds true or false.

Example:

```cpp
int age = 25;
float temperature = 36.5;
char grade = 'A';
bool isStudent = true;
```

4. **Operators**

- o Operators perform operations on variables and values.
- o **Arithmetic Operators**: +, -, *, /, %.
- o **Relational Operators**: ==, !=, <, >, <=, >=.
- o **Logical Operators**: &&, ||, !.

Example:

cpp

```
int a = 5, b = 10;
cout << "Sum: " << a + b << endl;      // Sum: 15
cout << "Is equal? " << (a == b) << endl; // Is equal? 0 (false)
```

Real-World Example: Age Checker

Let's create a simple program that uses variables, conditional statements, and basic input/output to check if a user is an adult.

cpp

```
#include <iostream>
using namespace std;

int main() {
    int age;
    cout << "Enter your age: ";
    cin >> age;

    if (age >= 18) {
```

```
    cout << "You are an adult." << endl;
} else {
    cout << "You are a minor." << endl;
}

    return 0;
}
```

Explanation:

- **cin >> age;**: cin is used to receive user input.
- **if (age >= 18)**: This conditional statement checks if the entered age is 18 or above, printing either "You are an adult" or "You are a minor."

Key Takeaways

- **C++ is a versatile, powerful language** with a wide range of applications.
- **Setting up the environment** is essential to start coding.
- **Basic syntax**: Understanding code structure, variables, and operators sets the foundation for further learning.
- **Writing and running simple programs** like "Hello, World!" and an age checker builds confidence and reinforces the concepts.

CHAPTER 2: VARIABLES, DATA TYPES, AND OPERATORS

Objective

This chapter focuses on the fundamental building blocks of programming: variables, data types, and operators. These concepts are essential for managing data in a program, allowing us to store, manipulate, and interact with information effectively. By the end of this chapter, readers will understand how to define variables, use different data types, and apply various operators. We'll also create a simple program to calculate the area of a rectangle using variables.

What Are Variables?

In programming, a ***variable*** is a named storage location in memory that holds a value. Variables are essential because they allow a program to remember information, which can then be used, modified, or displayed.

- **Naming Variables**: Choose descriptive names that indicate what the variable represents. For example, length and width are good names for rectangle dimensions.
- **Declaration and Initialization**: When you create a variable, you declare its data type and can optionally assign an initial value.

Example:

cpp
Copy code

```
int age = 20;      // declares an integer variable named age
```
with an initial value of 20
```
double price = 9.99; // declares a double variable named
```
price with an initial value of 9.99

Data Types

Data types specify what kind of data a variable can hold. C++ has several primary data types:

1. **Integer Types**:
   - **int**: Stores whole numbers (e.g., -5, 10, 1000).
   - **short**, **long**, and **long long**: Variants of int for storing smaller or larger numbers.
   - Example:

     cpp
     Copy code
     ```
     int count = 100;
     long distance = 1000000L;
     ```

2. **Floating-Point Types**:
   - **float**: Stores single-precision decimal numbers, suitable for lower precision (e.g., 3.14).

- o **double**: Stores double-precision decimal numbers, preferred for more accurate calculations.
- o Example:

cpp
Copy code
float temperature = 36.6f;
double price = 19.99;

3. **Character Type**:
   - o **char**: Holds a single character or ASCII value (e.g., 'A', '1', '%').
   - o Characters are enclosed in single quotes ('), whereas strings use double quotes (").
   - o Example:

cpp
Copy code
char grade = 'A';

4. **Boolean Type**:
   - o **bool**: Stores true or false values.
   - o Useful for conditions and logical operations.
   - o Example:

cpp
bool isStudent = true;

5. **String Type** (not a primitive type, but widely used):

    o   **string**: Holds a sequence of characters (like words or sentences). Requires the #include <string> header.

    o   Example:

    cpp

    Copy code

    ```
    #include <string>
    string name = "Alice";
    ```

Operators in C++

Operators are symbols that perform operations on variables or values. C++ offers several types of operators:

1. **Arithmetic Operators**

    o   Used for basic mathematical calculations.

    o   Examples:

        ▪   + (addition): Adds two values.

        ▪   - (subtraction): Subtracts one value from another.

        ▪   * (multiplication): Multiplies two values.

        ▪   / (division): Divides one value by another.

        ▪   % (modulus): Returns the remainder of a division.

    Example:

cpp

Copy code

```cpp
int x = 10;
int y = 3;
int sum = x + y;      // sum is 13
int difference = x - y; // difference is 7
int product = x * y;   // product is 30
int quotient = x / y;  // quotient is 3
int remainder = x % y;  // remainder is 1
```

2. **Relational Operators**
   - Compare values and return true or false.
   - Examples:
     - == (equal to)
     - != (not equal to)
     - < (less than)
     - > (greater than)
     - <= (less than or equal to)
     - >= (greater than or equal to)

Example:

cpp

```cpp
int a = 5;
int b = 10;
bool result = a < b; // result is true
```

3. **Logical Operators**
   - Combine multiple conditions.
   - Examples:
     - && (logical AND): true if both conditions are true.
     - || (logical OR): true if at least one condition is true.
     - ! (logical NOT): Inverts the truth value.

Example:

```cpp
bool isSunny = true;
bool hasUmbrella = false;
bool goOutside = isSunny && !hasUmbrella; // goOutside is true
```

4. **Assignment Operators**
   - Assign values to variables.
   - = (simple assignment), +=, -=, *=, /=, etc., modify the variable by performing an operation with its current value.

Example:

```cpp
int count = 10;
```

count += 5; // count is now 15

Example Program: Calculating the Area of a Rectangle

Now that we understand variables, data types, and operators, let's put them into practice by calculating the area of a rectangle. This example will use variables for length and width and apply the multiplication operator.

1. **Problem Statement**

   o We want a program where the user can enter the length and width of a rectangle. The program will then calculate and display the area of the rectangle.

2. **Plan**

   o Declare two variables for length and width (use float for potential decimal values).

   o Get user input for length and width.

   o Calculate the area using the formula: area = length * width.

   o Display the result.

3. **Code**

```cpp
#include <iostream>
using namespace std;

int main() {
```

```cpp
// Declare variables for length, width, and area
float length, width, area;

// Get user input
cout << "Enter the length of the rectangle: ";
cin >> length;
cout << "Enter the width of the rectangle: ";
cin >> width;

// Calculate the area
area = length * width;

// Display the result
cout << "The area of the rectangle is: " << area << endl;

return 0;
}
```

4. **Code Explanation**

   o **float length, width, area;**: Declares three float variables to store length, width, and area. We use float in case the user enters decimal values.

   o **cin >> length; and cin >> width;**: cin takes input from the user and stores it in length and width.

- o **area = length * width;**: This line calculates the area of the rectangle by multiplying length and width and stores the result in area.
- o **cout << area**: Outputs the result to the console.

5. **Sample Run**

yaml

Enter the length of the rectangle: 5.5

Enter the width of the rectangle: 2.3

The area of the rectangle is: 12.65

Practice Exercises

To reinforce these concepts, here are a few exercises you can try:

1. **Calculate the Perimeter of a Rectangle**: Modify the area program to calculate the perimeter using the formula perimeter = 2 * (length + width).
2. **Temperature Conversion**: Write a program that converts temperatures from Celsius to Fahrenheit.
3. **Simple Interest Calculator**: Write a program that calculates simple interest using the formula interest = principal * rate * time.

- **Variables** are containers for storing data that can be modified during a program's execution.
- **Data Types** define the kind of data a variable can hold, such as integers, decimals, characters, and booleans.
- **Operators** allow us to perform calculations and make logical comparisons, essential for decision-making in code.

In this chapter, we covered the basics of variables, data types, and operators, which form the foundation of data handling in C++. Next, we'll dive into control structures, which allow programs to make decisions and repeat actions based on conditions.

CHAPTER 3: CONTROL STRUCTURES – CONDITIONS AND LOOPS

Objective

This chapter introduces control structures, which allow programs to make decisions and repeat tasks. We'll explore conditional statements like if, else, and switch, as well as loops (for, while, and do-while) that let us execute code multiple times based on conditions. By the end of this chapter, readers will be able to build a basic calculator and a number guessing game.

Conditional Statements

Conditional statements enable a program to take different actions based on conditions, which are evaluated as true or false.

1. **The if Statement**
   o The if statement checks a condition and executes code only if the condition is true.

Example:

```cpp
int age = 18;
if (age >= 18) {
    cout << "You are eligible to vote." << endl;
}
```

2. **The else Statement**

   o The else statement provides an alternative action if the if condition is false.

   Example:

   cpp
   ```
   int age = 16;
   if (age >= 18) {
       cout << "You are eligible to vote." << endl;
   } else {
       cout << "You are not eligible to vote." << endl;
   }
   ```

3. **The else if Statement**

   o else if allows for multiple conditions in a sequence, providing different actions for each condition.

   Example:

   cpp
   ```
   int score = 85;
   if (score >= 90) {
       cout << "Grade: A" << endl;
   } else if (score >= 80) {
       cout << "Grade: B" << endl;
   } else if (score >= 70) {
   ```

```cpp
    cout << "Grade: C" << endl;
} else {
    cout << "Grade: F" << endl;
}
```

4. **The switch Statement**

   o   The switch statement allows a variable to be tested against a list of values, executing different code blocks depending on the value.

Example:

```cpp
cpp
int choice = 2;
switch (choice) {
    case 1:
        cout << "You chose option 1." << endl;
        break;
    case 2:
        cout << "You chose option 2." << endl;
        break;
    default:
        cout << "Invalid choice." << endl;
        break;
}
```

o **Note**: Each case block ends with break; to prevent "fall-through" behavior (where subsequent cases would also execute).

Loops

Loops allow a program to repeat actions multiple times. C++ has three main types of loops: for, while, and do-while.

1. **The for Loop**

   o A for loop is generally used when the number of iterations is known.

   o Syntax: for (initialization; condition; update)

Example: Print numbers from 1 to 5.

cpp

```
for (int i = 1; i <= 5; i++) {
    cout << i << " ";
}
```

   o Here, int i = 1 initializes i, i <= 5 is the condition, and i++ increments i after each loop.

2. **The while Loop**

   o A while loop continues executing as long as its condition remains true. It's useful when the number of iterations isn't known in advance.

Example:

cpp

int count = 1;

while (count <= 5) {

    cout << count << " ";

    count++;

}

3. **The do-while Loop**

   o   Similar to a while loop, but it always executes at least
       once because the condition is checked after the loop
       body.

Example:

cpp

int count = 1;

do {

    cout << count << " ";

    count++;

} while (count <= 5);

Example 1: Basic Calculator

Let's create a simple calculator that performs basic arithmetic
operations (+, -, *, /) based on user input. The program will prompt

the user for two numbers and an operator, perform the operation, and display the result.

1. **Problem Statement**

   o Prompt the user for two numbers and an operator.

   o Use if-else or switch to perform the appropriate arithmetic operation.

   o Display the result.

2. **Code**

```cpp
cpp
#include <iostream>
using namespace std;

int main() {
    double num1, num2;
    char op;

    // Get input from the user
    cout << "Enter the first number: ";
    cin >> num1;
    cout << "Enter an operator (+, -, *, /): ";
    cin >> op;
    cout << "Enter the second number: ";
    cin >> num2;
```

```cpp
// Perform the operation using if-else statements
if (op == '+') {
    cout << "Result: " << num1 + num2 << endl;
} else if (op == '-') {
    cout << "Result: " << num1 - num2 << endl;
} else if (op == '*') {
    cout << "Result: " << num1 * num2 << endl;
} else if (op == '/') {
    if (num2 != 0) {
        cout << "Result: " << num1 / num2 << endl;
    } else {
        cout << "Error: Division by zero!" << endl;
    }
} else {
    cout << "Invalid operator!" << endl;
}

return 0;
}
```

3. **Explanation**

   o **User Input**: cin >> num1 and cin >> num2 receive numbers, and cin >> op gets the operator.

   o **Conditional Statements**: The if-else structure checks the operator (+, -, *, or /) and performs the operation. Division checks that num2 isn't zero to avoid division errors.

Example 2: Number Guessing Game

This game will generate a random number between 1 and 100, and the user has to guess the number. After each guess, the program will tell the user if the guess was too high or too low. The game continues until the correct number is guessed.

1. **Problem Statement**
   - Generate a random number between 1 and 100.
   - Use a while loop to keep asking for guesses.
   - Provide feedback after each guess.
   - End the loop when the user guesses correctly.

2. **Code**

```cpp
#include <iostream>
#include <cstdlib> // For rand() and srand()
#include <ctime>   // For time()
using namespace std;

int main() {
    srand(time(0)); // Seed the random number generator
    int target = rand() % 100 + 1; // Generate a random number
between 1 and 100
```

```cpp
    int guess;
    int attempts = 0;

    cout << "Welcome to the Number Guessing Game!" <<
endl;
    cout << "Guess a number between 1 and 100: ";

    // Loop until the correct number is guessed
    while (true) {
        cin >> guess;
        attempts++;

        if (guess > target) {
            cout << "Too high! Try again: ";
        } else if (guess < target) {
            cout << "Too low! Try again: ";
        } else {
            cout << "Congratulations! You guessed the number
in " << attempts << " attempts." << endl;
            break;
        }
    }

    return 0;
}
```

3. **Explanation**

   o **Random Number Generation**: rand() % 100 + 1 generates a random number between 1 and 100. srand(time(0)); seeds the random number generator based on the current time.

   o **Loop and Feedback**: The while (true) loop continues until the user guesses the correct number. Each guess is compared to target, providing feedback if it's too high, too low, or correct.

   o **Ending the Game**: When the guess is correct, the program outputs the number of attempts and exits the loop with break.

Practice Exercises

1. **Odd or Even Checker**: Write a program that asks the user for a number and tells them if it's odd or even.

2. **Multiplication Table**: Create a program that prints the multiplication table for a number entered by the user.

3. **Countdown Timer**: Ask the user for a number and use a while loop to count down to zero, displaying each number.

- **Conditional Statements** (if, else, switch) allow programs to make decisions based on conditions.
- **Loops** (for, while, do-while) enable repeated execution of code, either a set number of times or while a condition remains true.
- **Practical Applications**: Building interactive programs like calculators and games makes use of these control structures, making programs dynamic and responsive to user input.

Control structures provide the flexibility for programs to behave differently based on conditions and user input, which is essential for building interactive and dynamic applications. In the next chapter, we'll delve into functions and modular programming to improve code organization and reusability.

CHAPTER 4: FUNCTIONS AND MODULAR PROGRAMMING

Objective

In this chapter, we'll introduce functions, which are reusable blocks of code designed to perform specific tasks. Functions help organize and modularize code, making programs easier to read, debug, and maintain. By the end of this chapter, readers will understand function syntax, how to define and call functions, and how modular programming can simplify complex tasks. We'll work through examples like calculating factorials and Fibonacci sequences using functions.

What is a Function?

A *function* is a named block of code that performs a specific task. Once defined, a function can be called or executed multiple times in a program without rewriting the code. Functions make it easier to manage larger codebases by breaking complex tasks into smaller, more manageable parts.

- **Syntax**:

```cpp
Copy code
return_type function_name(parameters) {
    // Function body
    return value; // Optional, depending on
return_type
}
```

- o **return_type**: Specifies the type of value the function returns (e.g., int, double, void if it returns nothing).

- o **function_name**: The name of the function, used to call it.

- o **parameters**: Optional inputs the function can take, enclosed in parentheses. Parameters allow data to be passed into the function.

- o **return**: If the function returns a value, the return statement specifies that value.

Benefits of Functions

1. **Reusability**: Write once, use multiple times without duplicating code.

2. **Modularity**: Breaks down a program into smaller, manageable parts.

3. **Clarity and Maintainability**: Organized code is easier to read, understand, and maintain.

4. **Debugging**: Isolated blocks of code make it easier to locate and fix issues.

Defining and Calling Functions

Let's create a simple function to illustrate the syntax and calling process.

1. **Defining a Function**
   - Below is a function that takes two integers as input and returns their sum:

```cpp
Copy code
int add(int a, int b) {
    return a + b;
}
```

   - **Explanation**: The add function has a return type of int and two int parameters (a and b). It returns the sum of these two integers.

2. **Calling a Function**
   - Once defined, the function can be called with arguments:

```cpp
Copy code
int result = add(5, 7); // Calls add with
arguments 5 and 7, result is 12
cout << "The sum is: " << result << endl;
```

3. **Functions with No Parameters and No Return**
   - Some functions don't require inputs or return values. For example:

```cpp
Copy code
void greet() {
    cout << "Hello, welcome to the program!" <<
endl;
}

// Calling the function
greet();
```

   - Here, void means the function returns nothing, and greet is called without any parameters.

Example 1: Calculating Factorial Using a Function

The factorial of a number n (denoted n!) is the product of all positive integers less than or equal to n. For example, $5! = 5 * 4 * 3 * 2 * 1 = 120$.

1. **Problem Statement**
   o Write a function that takes an integer n as input and returns its factorial.
2. **Code**

```cpp
Copy code
#include <iostream>
using namespace std;

// Function to calculate factorial
int factorial(int n) {
    int result = 1;
    for (int i = 1; i <= n; i++) {
        result *= i;
    }
    return result;
}

int main() {
    int number;
    cout << "Enter a number to find its
factorial: ";
    cin >> number;

    int fact = factorial(number); // Calling
the factorial function
    cout << "Factorial of " << number << " is "
<< fact << endl;

    return 0;
}
```

3. **Explanation**
    o **factorial Function**: This function calculates the factorial of a number using a for loop, iterating from 1 to n and multiplying each value.
    o **Calling the Function**: The main program calls factorial(number), which returns the result to fact and displays it.

Example 2: Generating Fibonacci Sequence Using a Function

The Fibonacci sequence is a series where each number is the sum of the two preceding ones, starting from 0 and 1. The first few numbers in the Fibonacci sequence are 0, 1, 1, 2, 3, 5, 8, ...

1. **Problem Statement**
    o Write a function that generates the first n numbers in the Fibonacci sequence.
2. **Code**

```cpp
Copy code
#include <iostream>
using namespace std;

// Function to generate Fibonacci sequence
void generateFibonacci(int n) {
    int a = 0, b = 1, next;

    cout << "Fibonacci sequence up to " << n <<
" terms: ";
    for (int i = 1; i <= n; i++) {
        cout << a << " ";
        next = a + b;
        a = b;
        b = next;
    }
    cout << endl;
```

```
}

int main() {
    int terms;
    cout << "Enter the number of terms in the
Fibonacci sequence: ";
    cin >> terms;

    generateFibonacci(terms); // Calling the
generateFibonacci function

    return 0;
}
```

3. **Explanation**

   o **generateFibonacci Function**: This function takes an integer n and prints the first n terms in the Fibonacci sequence. It uses variables a and b to store the two preceding numbers and calculates the next number as their sum.

   o **Calling the Function**: In the main function, generateFibonacci is called with the number of terms, displaying the sequence.

Modular Programming and Code Organization

Modular programming is a design approach where a program is divided into smaller parts, or modules. Each module is a self-contained piece of code with a specific function, enhancing readability, reusability, and maintainability.

1. **Splitting Large Tasks into Smaller Functions**

o For instance, if you're building a calculator, you might have separate functions for addition, subtraction, multiplication, and division. This modular approach keeps the code organized and easy to debug.

2. **Minimizing Repeated Code**

o Functions allow you to write code once and reuse it throughout the program. For example, if you're using factorial calculations in multiple places, defining a factorial function once saves time and reduces errors.

3. **Example of a Modular Program**

o Below is a simple modular program that combines factorial and Fibonacci functions:

```cpp
Copy code
#include <iostream>
using namespace std;

int factorial(int n) {
    int result = 1;
    for (int i = 1; i <= n; i++) {
        result *= i;
    }
    return result;
}

void generateFibonacci(int n) {
    int a = 0, b = 1, next;
    cout << "Fibonacci sequence: ";
    for (int i = 1; i <= n; i++) {
        cout << a << " ";
        next = a + b;
        a = b;
        b = next;
```

```
    }
    cout << endl;
}

int main() {
    int choice, number;

    cout << "Choose an option:" << endl;
    cout << "1. Calculate Factorial" << endl;
    cout << "2. Generate Fibonacci Sequence" <<
endl;
    cin >> choice;

    cout << "Enter a number: ";
    cin >> number;

    if (choice == 1) {
        cout << "Factorial of " << number << "
is " << factorial(number) << endl;
    } else if (choice == 2) {
        generateFibonacci(number);
    } else {
        cout << "Invalid choice." << endl;
    }

    return 0;
}
```

o **Explanation**:

- The main function displays a menu and prompts the user to choose between calculating a factorial or generating a Fibonacci sequence.

- Based on the choice, it calls the relevant function, factorial or `generateFibonacci`.

Practice Exercises

1. **Prime Number Checker**: Write a function that checks if a given number is prime.
2. **Power Function**: Write a function that calculates base^exponent using a loop.
3. **Temperature Converter**: Write two functions, one for converting Celsius to Fahrenheit and another for Fahrenheit to Celsius.

- **Functions** are reusable blocks of code that perform specific tasks, making code modular and organized.
- **Syntax and Structure**: Functions have a return type, a name, parameters, and a body.
- **Modular Programming** divides complex tasks into smaller functions, making code easier to understand, maintain, and debug.

With functions, we can build modular and organized programs, an essential skill as projects grow in complexity. In the next chapter, we'll move on to arrays, which allow us to manage collections of data efficiently within a single variable.

CHAPTER 5: ARRAYS AND BASIC DATA HANDLING

Objective

This chapter introduces arrays, a data structure that allows us to store multiple values of the same type within a single variable. We'll cover how to declare, initialize, and access arrays, along with basic operations. By the end, readers will be able to create a program that stores and analyzes a list of test scores.

What is an Array?

An *array* is a collection of elements of the same data type stored in a contiguous block of memory. Each element in an array is accessed using an index, starting from 0. Arrays are useful when working with collections of data that require efficient storage and easy access.

For example, if we need to store multiple test scores, instead of creating separate variables for each score, we can use an array.

- **Syntax**:

```cpp
Copy code
data_type array_name[array_size];
```

  - o **data_type**: Specifies the type of elements (e.g., int, float, char).
  - o **array_name**: The name of the array.
  - o **array_size**: The number of elements the array can hold.

Declaring and Initializing Arrays

1. **Declaration Without Initialization**

   Declaring an array allocates memory but doesn't set any values.

   ```cpp
   Copy code
   int scores[5];
   ```

   - This line declares an integer array scores with space for 5 elements.

2. **Declaration with Initialization**

   We can initialize arrays at the time of declaration by providing values in curly braces.

   ```cpp
   Copy code
   int scores[5] = {90, 85, 78, 92, 88};
   ```

   - This initializes scores with five values. The array length is automatically set to 5 based on the number of values provided.

3. **Accessing Array Elements**

   Array elements are accessed using indices, starting from 0. For example:

   ```cpp
   Copy code
   cout << "First score: " << scores[0] << endl;
   ```

4. **Modifying Array Elements**

Array elements can be updated by assigning new values to specific indices.

```cpp
Copy code
scores[1] = 89; // Changes the second score from 85 to 89
```

Basic Operations on Arrays

1. **Looping Through an Array**

Loops are commonly used to iterate over arrays, allowing us to access and manipulate each element. Here's an example of using a for loop to display all scores:

```cpp
Copy code
for (int i = 0; i < 5; i++) {
    cout << "Score " << (i + 1) << ": " << scores[i] << endl;
}
```

2. **Calculating the Sum of Array Elements**

Adding up all the elements in an array is a typical operation when calculating averages or totals.

```cpp
Copy code
int sum = 0;
for (int i = 0; i < 5; i++) {
    sum += scores[i];
```

}

3. Finding the Maximum and Minimum Values in an Array

We can find the highest and lowest scores by iterating through the array and comparing each element.

```cpp
Copy code
int max_score = scores[0];
int min_score = scores[0];
for (int i = 1; i < 5; i++) {
   if (scores[i] > max_score) {
      max_score = scores[i];
   }
   if (scores[i] < min_score) {
      min_score = scores[i];
   }
}
```

4. Calculating the Average of Array Elements

Once we have the sum, we can calculate the average by dividing it by the number of elements.

```cpp
Copy code
double average = static_cast<double>(sum) / 5;
```

Example Program: Storing and Analyzing Test Scores

Now, let's create a program that stores a series of test scores and performs basic analysis by calculating the sum, average, maximum, and minimum scores.

1. **Problem Statement**
   o The program should store a list of test scores, calculate the total and average, and identify the highest and lowest scores.
2. **Code**

cpp
Copy code

```cpp
#include <iostream>
using namespace std;

int main() {
    const int SIZE = 5; // Number of scores
    int scores[SIZE];   // Array to store scores
    int sum = 0, max_score, min_score;

    // Input scores from the user
    cout << "Enter " << SIZE << " test scores:" << endl;
    for (int i = 0; i < SIZE; i++) {
        cout << "Score " << (i + 1) << ": ";
        cin >> scores[i];
        sum += scores[i];
    }

    // Initialize max and min scores
    max_score = scores[0];
    min_score = scores[0];

    // Find max and min scores
    for (int i = 1; i < SIZE; i++) {
        if (scores[i] > max_score) {
            max_score = scores[i];
        }
        if (scores[i] < min_score) {
            min_score = scores[i];
        }
    }
```

```cpp
// Calculate the average
double average = static_cast<double>(sum) / SIZE;

// Display results
cout << "\nSummary of Test Scores:" << endl;
cout << "Total: " << sum << endl;
cout << "Average: " << average << endl;
cout << "Highest Score: " << max_score << endl;
cout << "Lowest Score: " << min_score << endl;

return 0;
}
```

3. **Explanation**

   o **Array Declaration**: We declare an integer array scores of size 5 to store test scores.

   o **Input Loop**: We prompt the user to enter each score, storing it in the array and updating the sum variable.

   o **Finding Maximum and Minimum**: We initialize max_score and min_score with the first score, then iterate through the array to find the highest and lowest scores.

   o **Calculating Average**: We divide the total sum by the number of scores to get the average.

   o **Displaying Results**: Finally, we print the total, average, highest, and lowest scores.

4. **Sample Output**

   yaml
   Copy code

Enter 5 test scores:
Score 1: 85
Score 2: 90
Score 3: 78
Score 4: 88
Score 5: 92

Summary of Test Scores:
Total: 433
Average: 86.6
Highest Score: 92
Lowest Score: 78

Practice Exercises

1. **Temperature Recorder**: Write a program that stores daily temperatures for a week in an array, then calculates and displays the highest, lowest, and average temperatures.

2. **Reversing an Array**: Write a function that takes an integer array and its size as arguments and prints the elements in reverse order.

3. **Even and Odd Counter**: Write a program that stores a list of integers in an array and counts how many are even and how many are odd.

- **Arrays** allow you to store multiple values of the same type in a single variable, which is useful for handling collections of data.

- **Accessing and Modifying Elements**: Array elements are accessed using indices, and their values can be updated as needed.

- **Common Operations**: Iterating, summing, finding maximum and minimum, and calculating averages are standard operations with arrays.

With arrays, you can efficiently handle collections of data and perform operations on each element, an essential skill for data handling in programming. In the next chapter, we'll introduce pointers and memory management, which are crucial for working with data at a deeper level in C++.

CHAPTER 6: POINTERS AND MEMORY MANAGEMENT

Objective

This chapter covers pointers, a powerful feature in C++ that allows direct access and manipulation of memory. We'll introduce basic pointer concepts, memory allocation using new and delete, and essential practices for memory safety. By the end, readers will be able to use pointers to dynamically allocate memory, particularly for arrays.

What is a Pointer?

A *pointer* is a variable that stores the memory address of another variable. Instead of storing a value directly, pointers store the location in memory where the value is kept, allowing us to manipulate data at its source. Understanding pointers is essential for dynamic memory management, working with data structures, and efficient memory usage.

- **Syntax**:

  cpp
  data_type* pointer_name;

- o **data_type**: Specifies the type of data the pointer will point to.
- o *: The asterisk denotes that this variable is a pointer.
- o **pointer_name**: The name of the pointer.

Declaring and Using Pointers

1. **Declaring a Pointer**

cpp

```
int* ptr; // Declares a pointer to an int
```

- o This pointer, ptr, can hold the memory address of an integer variable.

2. **Assigning an Address to a Pointer**

Use the *address-of* operator (&) to obtain the memory address of a variable and store it in a pointer.

cpp

```
int num = 10;
int* ptr = &num; // ptr now holds the address of num
```

3. **Dereferencing a Pointer**

The *dereference* operator (*) allows us to access or modify the value at the memory address stored in the pointer.

```cpp
cout << *ptr; // Outputs 10 (value of num)
*ptr = 20;   // Changes num to 20
```

Dynamic Memory Allocation

Static arrays have a fixed size determined at compile time, but sometimes, we don't know the required size until runtime. *Dynamic memory allocation* enables us to allocate memory during program execution, and pointers are essential for this.

- **Using new**: The new keyword dynamically allocates memory for a variable or an array, returning a pointer to the allocated memory.

  ```cpp
  int* ptr = new int;      // Allocates memory for a single integer
  int* arr = new int[10];  // Allocates memory for an array of 10 integers
  ```

- **Using delete**: The delete keyword releases dynamically allocated memory, helping prevent memory leaks (unused memory that was never released).

  ```cpp
  delete ptr;   // Frees memory allocated for the single integer
  delete[] arr; // Frees memory allocated for the array
  ```

Example: Dynamic Memory Allocation for an Array

Let's create a program that allows the user to enter a list of scores. The number of scores is determined at runtime, so we'll use dynamic memory allocation to create an array that fits precisely.

1. **Problem Statement**
   - Prompt the user to enter the number of scores.
   - Allocate memory dynamically for an array of that size.
   - Allow the user to input each score, then calculate the average score.
   - Release the allocated memory when done.

2. **Code**

```cpp
#include <iostream>
using namespace std;

int main() {
    int numScores;

    // Get the number of scores from the user
    cout << "Enter the number of scores: ";
    cin >> numScores;

    // Dynamically allocate memory for an array of scores
```

```cpp
    int* scores = new int[numScores];

    // Input scores from the user
    cout << "Enter the scores:" << endl;
    for (int i = 0; i < numScores; i++) {
        cout << "Score " << (i + 1) << ": ";
        cin >> scores[i];
    }
    // Calculate the average score
    int sum = 0;
    for (int i = 0; i < numScores; i++) {
        sum += scores[i];
    }
    double average = static_cast<double>(sum) / numScores;

    // Display the average score
    cout << "The average score is: " << average << endl;

    // Free the dynamically allocated memory
    delete[] scores;

    return 0;
}
```

3. **Explanation**

- o **Dynamic Allocation**: int* scores = new int[numScores]; dynamically allocates an array of integers with a size determined by the user.
- o **Calculating the Average**: We sum all the scores in the array and calculate the average.
- o **Memory Deallocation**: delete[] scores; releases the allocated memory, ensuring no memory leak occurs.

4. **Sample Output**

yaml

Enter the number of scores: 3

Enter the scores:

Score 1: 85

Score 2: 90

Score 3: 78

The average score is: 84.3333

Memory Safety Tips

When working with pointers and dynamic memory, several practices help maintain memory safety and prevent bugs.

1. **Always Initialize Pointers**
   - o Uninitialized pointers contain random memory addresses, which can lead to crashes or unpredictable behavior. Initialize pointers to nullptr when declaring them:

```cpp
cpp
int* ptr = nullptr;
```

2. Check for Null Pointers

o Before using a pointer, verify it's not null to avoid dereferencing a null pointer.

```cpp
cpp
if (ptr != nullptr) {
    // Safe to use ptr
}
```

3. Free Dynamically Allocated Memory

o Always delete dynamically allocated memory to prevent memory leaks.

4. Avoid Dangling Pointers

o A *dangling pointer* points to memory that's been freed. After delete, set the pointer to nullptr to avoid accidental use.

```cpp
cpp
delete ptr;
ptr = nullptr;
```

5. Limit Pointer Usage in Simple Programs

o Although pointers are powerful, avoid overusing them, especially in simpler code where regular variables can suffice. Pointers are best suited for dynamic memory management and data structures, such as linked lists and trees.

Advantages of Dynamic Memory Allocation

1. **Flexibility**: Allocate only as much memory as needed, based on user input or runtime conditions.
2. **Efficiency**: Save memory by allocating only when required and deallocating when done.
3. **Scalability**: Dynamic allocation is critical for handling data structures that grow and shrink, like arrays that can't be resized without reallocation.

Practice Exercises

1. **Dynamic Array Resizing**: Create a program that dynamically allocates an array, stores values, and allows the user to resize the array (doubling its size) if more space is needed.
2. **Memory Management with Multiple Pointers**: Write a program that dynamically allocates memory for two arrays, performs operations on them, and then correctly deallocates the memory.
3. **Pointer Swap Function**: Write a function that takes two integer pointers as arguments and swaps their values.

- **Pointers**: Variables that store memory addresses, allowing direct access to memory.
- **Dynamic Memory Allocation**: The new and delete keywords let us allocate and free memory at runtime, providing flexibility and control over memory usage.
- **Memory Safety**: Proper pointer handling, initializing pointers, and deallocating memory are crucial to preventing memory leaks and errors.

Pointers and dynamic memory management are core features of C++ that allow for efficient and flexible memory use, especially in larger applications where memory requirements change dynamically. In the next chapter, we'll explore strings and string manipulation, applying pointers in managing character arrays and more complex data handling.

CHAPTER 7: STRINGS AND STRING MANIPULATION

Objective

In this chapter, we'll explore strings in C++, covering basic operations and functions that make working with text easy and efficient. Strings are essential for handling text data, and understanding how to manipulate them will enable readers to perform a variety of tasks, from formatting text to checking for patterns. By the end of this chapter, readers will be able to work with C++ strings and implement a program to check if a word is a palindrome or to reverse a string.

What is a String?

A *string* is a sequence of characters. In C++, there are two main ways to work with strings:

1. **C-style strings** (character arrays)
2. **Standard Library strings** (using the std::string class)

The std::string class is easier and more versatile than C-style strings, so it's generally recommended for most tasks.

Working with std::string

The std::string class, available through the #include <string> header, provides a flexible way to store and manipulate text in C++.

1. **Declaring and Initializing Strings**

cpp

```
#include <string>
using namespace std;
string str1 = "Hello";
string str2("World");
string str3 = str1 + " " + str2; // Concatenation
```

2. **Common String Operations**

   o **Concatenation**: Joining strings using the + operator.

      cpp

      ```
      string greeting = "Hello, " + name;
      ```

   o **Accessing Characters**: Use the [] operator or .at() method to access individual characters by index.

      cpp

      Copy code

      ```
      char firstChar = str1[0]; // Access first character
      char secondChar = str1.at(1); // Another way to access characters
      ```

   o **String Length**: Use .length() or .size() to get the number of characters in a string.

```cpp
int len = str1.length();
```

o **Comparing Strings**: The == operator checks if two strings are equal, while !=, <, and > operators compare them lexicographically.

```cpp
if (str1 == str2) { /* code */ }
```

3. **Modifying Strings**

o **Appending Text**: The .append() function adds text to the end of a string.

```cpp
str1.append(" there");
```

o **Inserting Text**: .insert() adds text at a specific position.

```cpp
str1.insert(0, "Say ");
```

o **Erasing Text**: .erase() removes characters starting from a specified index.

```cpp
str1.erase(0, 4); // Removes the first 4 characters
```

     o **Replacing Text**: .replace() substitutes part of a string with another substring.

cpp

```cpp
str1.replace(0, 5, "Hi");
```

String Functions and Utilities

1. **Substring Extraction**
   - o The .substr() function extracts a portion of a string starting at a specified index.

   cpp

   ```cpp
   string part = str1.substr(0, 5); // Gets the first 5 characters
   ```

2. **Finding Substrings**
   - o .find() searches for the first occurrence of a substring and returns the starting index or string::npos if not found.

   cpp

   ```cpp
   size_t pos = str1.find("world");
   if (pos != string::npos) {
       // Substring found at index pos
   }
   ```

3. **Converting Strings to Lowercase and Uppercase**

C++ doesn't have built-in string methods for case conversion, but we can use loops and toupper or tolower from <cctype>.

cpp

Copy code

```
#include <cctype>
for (char& c : str1) {
    c = tolower(c);
}
```

4. **String Reversal**

o   Use std::reverse from <algorithm> to reverse a string.

cpp

```
#include <algorithm>
reverse(str1.begin(), str1.end());
```

Example 1: Checking for a Palindrome

A *palindrome* is a word or phrase that reads the same forward and backward, ignoring spaces, punctuation, and capitalization. Examples include "madam" and "racecar."

1. **Problem Statement**
   - Write a program that checks if a string is a palindrome.

2. **Approach**
   - Convert the string to lowercase to ensure case insensitivity.
   - Use two indices (one from the start and one from the end) to compare characters.
   - Ignore non-alphanumeric characters.

3. **Code**

```cpp
cpp
#include <iostream>
#include <string>
#include <algorithm>
#include <cctype>
using namespace std;
bool isPalindrome(string str) {
    // Convert to lowercase and remove non-alphanumeric characters
    string filtered;
    for (char c : str) {
        if (isalnum(c)) {
            filtered += tolower(c);
        }
```

```cpp
    }


    // Check for palindrome
    int left = 0;
    int right = filtered.length() - 1;
    while (left < right) {
        if (filtered[left] != filtered[right]) {
            return false;
        }
        left++;
        right--;
    }
    return true;
}
int main() {
    string input;
    cout << "Enter a word or phrase: ";
    getline(cin, input);
    if (isPalindrome(input)) {
        cout << "\"" << input << "\" is a palindrome." << endl;
    } else {
        cout << "\"" << input << "\" is not a palindrome." <<
endl;
    }
```

```
    return 0;
}
```

4. **Explanation**

   o **Filtering Non-Alphanumeric Characters**: We build a new string with only alphanumeric characters converted to lowercase.

   o **Checking for Palindrome**: We compare characters from both ends, moving inward. If any pair doesn't match, the function returns false.

Example 2: Reversing a String

This example demonstrates how to reverse a string entered by the user.

1. **Problem Statement**

   o Write a program that reverses the input string.

2. **Approach**

   o Use std::reverse to reverse the string in place.

3. **Code**

```cpp
#include <iostream>
#include <string>
#include <algorithm>
using namespace std;
```

```
int main() {
    string input;
    cout << "Enter a word or phrase: ";
    getline(cin, input);

    // Reverse the string
    reverse(input.begin(), input.end());

    // Display the reversed string
    cout << "Reversed: " << input << endl;

    return 0;
}
```

4. **Explanation**
   o **Reversing the String**: std::reverse from `<algorithm>` takes two iterators (begin() and end()) and reverses the string in place.
   o **Displaying the Result**: We output the reversed string.

Practice Exercises

1. **Count Vowels and Consonants**: Write a program that counts the number of vowels and consonants in a string.

2. **Find and Replace Substring**: Create a program that finds a substring in a string and replaces it with another substring.

3. **Remove Whitespace**: Write a program that removes all spaces from a string.

- **Strings** are essential for working with text data, and C++ provides a robust std::string class with built-in methods for handling text.

- **Common Operations**: Concatenation, length, substring, and search operations are frequently used in string manipulation.

- **String Functions**: Functions like find, substr, and reverse make complex string operations easier.

- **Real-World Applications**: Checking for palindromes and reversing strings are practical examples that build string manipulation skills.

Strings are central to data handling and text processing, and mastering their manipulation enables you to create programs that process and interpret text effectively. In the next chapter, we'll cover structures, allowing us to group related data into custom data types for more organized data management

Chapter 8: Working with Structures

Objective

In this chapter, we'll learn about *structures* in C++, which provide a way to group related data of different types into a single unit. Structures are particularly useful for representing complex data, like a book in a library system, where different pieces of information (e.g., title, author, and publication year) are related. By the end of this chapter, readers will be able to create and use structures to organize data efficiently.

What is a Structure?

A *structure* (struct) in C++ is a user-defined data type that groups together variables of different types. Structures help represent real-world entities by combining data into a single, organized unit. Each variable in a structure is called a *member*.

- **Syntax**:

```cpp
struct StructName {
    data_type member1;
    data_type member2;
    // More members...
};
```

- o **struct StructName**: Defines a structure with a specified name (e.g., Book).
- o **Members**: Variables within the structure, each with its own data type.

Declaring and Using Structures

Let's define a structure to represent a book in a library.

1. **Defining a Structure**

   cpp
   ```
   struct Book {
       string title;
       string author;
       int publicationYear;
       double price;
   };
   ```

   - o This Book structure has four members: title and author (strings), publicationYear (integer), and price (double).

2. **Creating Structure Variables**

   Once the structure is defined, you can create variables of that structure type:

   cpp

Book book1;

Book book2;

3. Accessing Structure Members

Use the dot operator (.) to access or modify members of a structure variable.

cpp

```
book1.title = "The Great Gatsby";
book1.author = "F. Scott Fitzgerald";
book1.publicationYear = 1925;
book1.price = 10.99;

cout << "Title: " << book1.title << endl;
cout << "Author: " << book1.author << endl;
```

4. Initializing Structures

Structures can be initialized directly using curly braces:

cpp

```
Book book2 = {"1984", "George Orwell", 1949, 15.99};
```

- o This assigns values to title, author, publicationYear, and price in book2 in the order they are defined in the structure.

82

Example: Creating a Structure for a Book

Let's create a program to manage a list of books in a library system. The program will use a structure to store information about each book, allowing us to organize and display library records.

1. **Problem Statement**
   - Define a Book structure with members for title, author, publication year, and price.
   - Create an array of Book structures to store multiple books.
   - Allow the user to input details for each book and display the library records.
2. **Code**

```cpp
cpp
#include <iostream>
#include <string>
using namespace std;


// Define the Book structure
struct Book {
    string title;
    string author;
    int publicationYear;
    double price;
};
```

```cpp
// Function to display book information
void displayBook(const Book& book) {
    cout << "Title: " << book.title << endl;
    cout << "Author: " << book.author << endl;
    cout << "Publication Year: " << book.publicationYear << endl;
    cout << "Price: $" << book.price << endl;
    cout << "-----------------------" << endl;
}

int main() {
    const int librarySize = 3;  // Number of books to enter
    Book library[librarySize];  // Array of Book structures

    // Input details for each book
    for (int i = 0; i < librarySize; i++) {
        cout << "Enter details for book " << (i + 1) << ":" << endl;
        cout << "Title: ";
        getline(cin, library[i].title);
        cout << "Author: ";
        getline(cin, library[i].author);
        cout << "Publication Year: ";
        cin >> library[i].publicationYear;
```

```
        cout << "Price: ";
        cin >> library[i].price;
        cin.ignore(); // Ignore leftover newline
        cout << "-----------------------" << endl;
    }


    // Display all books in the library
    cout << "\nLibrary Records:" << endl;
    for (int i = 0; i < librarySize; i++) {
        displayBook(library[i]);
    }


    return 0;
}
```

3. **Explanation**

   o **Book Structure**: The Book structure holds details about each book.

   o **displayBook Function**: This function takes a Book reference and prints its details. Using a function simplifies displaying book information and makes the code modular.

   o **Array of Structures**: We create an array, library, to store multiple books.

o **User Input**: The program prompts the user to enter details for each book, then stores them in the array.

Why Structures Are Useful

Structures are useful for organizing related data under one unit, making complex data handling more manageable and readable.

1. **Data Grouping**: Structures allow logically related data to be grouped together. For example, the information about a book is stored in a single Book structure instead of multiple individual variables.

2. **Modularity and Reusability**: Structures promote modularity by enabling us to treat each structure as a separate unit. The Book structure can be reused in different parts of the program or in future programs.

3. **Simplified Code**: Structures keep code organized by associating related data under a single name, making it easier to understand and maintain.

4. **Real-World Applications**: Structures are ideal for representing real-world entities, such as books, students, employees, or products, where multiple pieces of data describe a single item.

Nested Structures

Structures can contain other structures as members, allowing even more complex data representations.

cpp

```cpp
struct Author {
    string name;
    int birthYear;
};

struct Book {
    string title;
    Author author; // Nested structure
    int publicationYear;
    double price;
};
```

- In this example, Author is a structure that holds an author's name and birth year. It's then used as a member within the Book structure to give additional details about the author of each book.

Practice Exercises

1. **Student Record System**: Create a Student structure with members for name, ID, and GPA. Write a program that stores multiple students and displays their records.
2. **Inventory Management**: Define a Product structure with members for name, quantity, and price. Use an array of Product structures to create an inventory system.

3. **Course Catalog**: Create a structure for a Course with members for course name, code, and credit hours. Write a program that allows the user to enter details for several courses and display them.

- **Structures** allow us to create custom data types that group related data, making complex data handling more manageable.
- **Members** of a structure can be of different data types, allowing us to represent diverse aspects of a real-world entity.
- **Arrays of Structures** let us organize multiple records, ideal for applications like library systems or inventory management.

Working with structures opens up a range of possibilities for organizing and managing complex data effectively, paving the way for building robust data-driven applications. In the next chapter, we'll dive into object-oriented programming, where we'll extend the concept of structures by adding functionality through classes and methods.

CHAPTER 9: INTRODUCTION TO OBJECT-ORIENTED PROGRAMMING (OOP)

Objective

This chapter introduces the fundamental concepts of Object-Oriented Programming (OOP) in C++, including classes, objects, and encapsulation. OOP allows us to create complex programs by modeling real-world entities through classes, which bundle data and functions into cohesive units. By the end of this chapter, readers will be able to define and use a class, specifically by creating a simple "Car" class with attributes and methods.

What is Object-Oriented Programming (OOP)?

Object-Oriented Programming (OOP) is a programming paradigm based on the concept of "objects," which can represent real-world entities with attributes (data) and behaviors (functions or methods). OOP organizes code by grouping related data and behavior, making it easier to design, understand, and maintain large programs.

Four Core Principles of OOP:

1. **Encapsulation**: Bundling data and methods within a class and restricting access to some components to protect the integrity of data.

2. **Abstraction**: Hiding the complex implementation details and exposing only essential features to the user.

3. **Inheritance**: Allowing new classes to derive properties and behaviors from existing classes, promoting code reuse.

4. **Polymorphism**: Enabling functions or methods to behave differently based on the object that calls them.

Classes and Objects

A *class* is a blueprint for creating objects, defining the attributes and behaviors that all objects of that type will share. An *object* is an instance of a class with its own specific data values.

1. **Defining a Class**

   o Classes are defined using the class keyword, with attributes (data members) and methods (member functions) enclosed within curly braces {}.

   cpp

   ```
   class ClassName {
       // Access specifier
   public:
       // Data members (attributes)
       // Member functions (methods)
   };
   ```

2. **Creating Objects**

    ○   Once a class is defined, we can create instances (objects) of the class by declaring variables of that class type.

cpp
ClassName objectName;

Example: Defining a "Car" Class

Let's create a "Car" class that represents different cars with specific attributes (such as brand, model, and speed) and behaviors (such as accelerating and braking).

1. **Class Definition**

```cpp
#include <iostream>
#include <string>
using namespace std;

class Car {
private:
    string brand;
    string model;
    int year;
    int speed;

public:
```

```cpp
    // Constructor to initialize attributes
    Car(string b, string m, int y) : brand(b), model(m), year(y),
speed(0) {}


    // Method to display car details
    void displayInfo() {
        cout << "Car: " << brand << " " << model << " (" <<
year << ")" << endl;
        cout << "Current speed: " << speed << " km/h" << endl;
    }


    // Method to accelerate
    void accelerate(int increment) {
        speed += increment;
        cout << "Accelerating by " << increment << " km/h.
New speed: " << speed << " km/h" << endl;
    }


    // Method to brake
    void brake(int decrement) {
        speed = (speed - decrement >= 0) ? speed - decrement :
0;
        cout << "Braking by " << decrement << " km/h. New
speed: " << speed << " km/h" << endl;
    }
```

};

2. **Explanation**

   o **Attributes (Data Members)**: The Car class has private attributes brand, model, year, and speed.

   o **Constructor**: The constructor Car(string b, string m, int y) initializes a car's brand, model, and year. The speed attribute is set to 0 by default.

   o **Methods (Member Functions)**:

   ▪ displayInfo(): Displays the car's details.

   ▪ accelerate(int increment): Increases the speed by a specified amount.

   ▪ brake(int decrement): Reduces the speed by a specified amount, ensuring it doesn't drop below 0.

3. **Encapsulation**

   o The Car class uses private attributes, enforcing encapsulation. Only methods within the class can directly access or modify the brand, model, year, and speed attributes.

   o The public methods (displayInfo, accelerate, brake) provide controlled access to the car's data.

Using the Car Class

With the Car class defined, we can create objects (instances of Car) and call their methods.

1. **Creating and Using a Car Object**

   cpp
   ```cpp
   int main() {
       // Create a Car object
       Car myCar("Toyota", "Camry", 2020);

       // Display car info
       myCar.displayInfo();

       // Accelerate and brake the car
       myCar.accelerate(30);  // Accelerate by 30 km/h
       myCar.brake(10);       // Brake by 10 km/h
       myCar.displayInfo();   // Display car info again

       return 0;
   }
   ```

2. **Output**

   bash
   ```bash
   Car: Toyota Camry (2020)
   ```

Current speed: 0 km/h

Accelerating by 30 km/h. New speed: 30 km/h

Braking by 10 km/h. New speed: 20 km/h

Car: Toyota Camry (2020)

Current speed: 20 km/h

Detailed Explanation of OOP Concepts in the Car Example

1. **Class and Object**:
   - The Car class serves as a blueprint, and myCar is an instance of this class with its own specific brand, model, year, and speed.

2. **Encapsulation**:
   - The attributes are marked as private, protecting them from direct access outside the class. Public methods control how these attributes are accessed and modified.

3. **Methods and Functionality**:
   - The accelerate and brake methods change the state of the car (i.e., the speed attribute), demonstrating how methods allow interaction with and modification of an object's state.

Benefits of OOP

1. **Modularity and Reusability**:
   - o Classes promote modularity by grouping related attributes and methods, making code easier to understand and reuse.

2. **Encapsulation for Data Protection**:
   - o Encapsulation hides the internal details of a class, exposing only the necessary methods for outside interaction. This safeguards data integrity by preventing unauthorized or accidental changes.

3. **Real-World Modeling**:
   - o OOP reflects real-world entities and interactions, making it easier to design applications with complex, interconnected parts.

4. **Code Maintenance**:
   - o OOP's modular design makes programs easier to update and maintain, especially as applications grow larger and more complex.

Practice Exercises

1. **Person Class**: Create a Person class with attributes like name, age, and address, and methods to display details and update the address.

2. **Bank Account Class**: Define a BankAccount class with attributes for the account holder's name, account balance, and account number. Implement methods to deposit, withdraw, and check the balance.

3. **Rectangle Class**: Write a Rectangle class with attributes for length and width, and methods to calculate the area and perimeter. Allow the user to change the dimensions.

- **Classes and Objects**: Classes are blueprints for creating objects that bundle data (attributes) and functionality (methods) into a cohesive unit.

- **Encapsulation**: Encapsulation restricts direct access to data within a class, enforcing controlled access and protecting data integrity.

- **OOP Benefits**: Object-oriented programming promotes modularity, reusability, and easy maintenance, making it an essential approach for building complex applications.

This chapter introduces the fundamental principles of OOP with a focus on classes, objects, and encapsulation. In the next chapter, we'll explore constructors, destructors, and the lifecycle of objects, providing deeper insight into how objects are created, used, and destroyed within a program.

Chapter 10: Constructors, Destructors, and Object Lifecycle

Objective

This chapter introduces constructors and destructors in C++, which manage the lifecycle of objects. Constructors allow for the automatic initialization of objects, while destructors handle cleanup when objects are no longer needed. By the end, readers will understand how to use constructors and destructors in a "Student" class to initialize and manage student data.

What are Constructors and Destructors?

1. **Constructor**: A *constructor* is a special function in a class that is automatically called when an object of that class is created. Its purpose is to initialize the object's attributes and allocate any necessary resources.

    o A constructor has the same name as the class and does not have a return type.

    o Constructors can be overloaded, allowing multiple constructors with different parameters.

2. **Destructor**: A *destructor* is a special function that is called automatically when an object goes out of scope or is explicitly deleted. It is primarily used to release resources

(like memory or file handles) that the object may have acquired during its lifetime.

- o A destructor has the same name as the class, prefixed with a tilde (~), and has no parameters or return type.
- o Each class has only one destructor.

The Object Lifecycle

The object lifecycle in C++ includes the following stages:

1. **Creation**: When an object is created, the constructor is called to initialize it.
2. **Usage**: The object performs tasks and interacts with other objects or functions.
3. **Destruction**: When the object goes out of scope or is explicitly deleted, the destructor is called to clean up resources.

Example: Building a "Student" Class with Constructors

Let's create a Student class with attributes such as name, age, and grade. We'll implement different types of constructors to initialize the student data and a destructor to handle cleanup if necessary.

1. **Class Definition**

```cpp
#include <iostream>
#include <string>
```

```cpp
using namespace std;

class Student {
private:
    string name;
    int age;
    char grade;
public:
    // Default Constructor
    Student() : name("Unknown"), age(0), grade('N') {
        cout << "Default constructor called. Student created with default values." << endl;
    }

    // Parameterized Constructor
    Student(string n, int a, char g) : name(n), age(a), grade(g)
    {
        cout << "Parameterized constructor called. Student created with specified values." << endl;
    }

    // Copy Constructor
    Student(const Student& other) : name(other.name), age(other.age), grade(other.grade) {
```

```
    cout << "Copy constructor called. Student copied from
another student object." << endl;
    }


    // Destructor
    ~Student() {
    cout << "Destructor called. Cleaning up student: " <<
name << endl;
    }


    // Method to display student information
    void displayInfo() const {
    cout << "Name: " << name << ", Age: " << age << ",
Grade: " << grade << endl;
    }
};
```

2. **Explanation**

   o **Default Constructor**: Student() initializes name,
   age, and grade with default values. This constructor
   is called when no arguments are provided.

   o **Parameterized Constructor**: Student(string n, int a,
   char g) initializes name, age, and grade with values
   provided by the user.

o **Copy Constructor**: Student(const Student& other) creates a new Student object as a copy of another Student object. This is used when creating a duplicate of an existing object.

o **Destructor**: ~Student() is called automatically when an object goes out of scope. It outputs a message to indicate the object is being destroyed. Here, it doesn't need to free any additional resources, but in more complex applications, it would be responsible for releasing resources like dynamic memory.

3. **Using the Student Class**

Now, let's create some Student objects using different constructors.

cpp

```
int main() {
    // Using the default constructor
    Student student1;
    student1.displayInfo();

    // Using the parameterized constructor
    Student student2("Alice", 20, 'A');
    student2.displayInfo();

    // Using the copy constructor
```

```
Student student3 = student2;
student3.displayInfo();

return 0;
}
```

4. **Expected Output**

yaml

Default constructor called. Student created with default values.

Name: Unknown, Age: 0, Grade: N

Parameterized constructor called. Student created with specified values.

Name: Alice, Age: 20, Grade: A

Copy constructor called. Student copied from another student object.

Name: Alice, Age: 20, Grade: A

Destructor called. Cleaning up student: Unknown

Destructor called. Cleaning up student: Alice

Destructor called. Cleaning up student: Alice

- o **Explanation**:
    - The default constructor initializes student1 with default values.

- The parameterized constructor initializes student2 with specified values.
- The copy constructor creates student3 as a copy of student2.
- When main exits, destructors are called for each Student object to indicate the end of their lifecycle.

Types of Constructors

1. **Default Constructor**: Initializes objects with default values. If no constructor is provided, C++ automatically generates a default constructor.

2. **Parameterized Constructor**: Takes arguments, allowing customized initialization. This is useful when specific values are needed at the time of object creation.

3. **Copy Constructor**: Creates a new object as a copy of an existing object. It's automatically called:
   o When an object is passed by value to a function.
   o When an object is returned by value from a function.
   o When initializing one object with another.

4. **Destructor**: Used to clean up resources when an object's lifecycle ends. It's essential when using dynamic memory or resources that require manual release.

Memory Management and Resource Cleanup

The constructor-destructor mechanism helps manage resources efficiently. Some key points for managing resources with constructors and destructors include:

1. **Allocating Resources in Constructors**: Resources (like dynamic memory or file handles) are typically allocated in constructors, ensuring that objects are initialized correctly before use.

   cpp

   Copy code

   ```
   int* data = new int[100]; // Dynamic allocation in constructor
   ```

2. **Releasing Resources in Destructors**: Any resource allocated in the constructor should be released in the destructor to avoid memory leaks.

   cpp

   Copy code

   ```
   delete[] data; // Deallocation in destructor
   ```

3. **RAII (Resource Acquisition is Initialization)**: This C++ idiom binds resource management to the object lifecycle. Resources are acquired in the constructor and released in the

destructor, making resource management automatic and exception-safe.

Practice Exercises

1. **Book Class with Constructors and Destructor**: Create a Book class with attributes for title, author, and price. Implement different constructors to initialize the class, including a copy constructor, and use a destructor to display a message when each Book object is destroyed.

2. **Rectangle Class with Dynamic Memory**: Write a Rectangle class that allocates dynamic memory for the length and width attributes in the constructor. Use the destructor to free the memory, ensuring no memory leaks.

3. **Course Class with Copy Constructor**: Design a Course class that includes a copy constructor. Use it to duplicate course details from one object to another, and verify that the destructor is called when the objects go out of scope.

- **Constructors**: Special functions that initialize an object's attributes and resources. They include default, parameterized, and copy constructors.

- **Destructors**: Automatically called when an object's lifecycle ends, cleaning up resources to avoid memory leaks.

- **Object Lifecycle**: The sequence of creation, usage, and destruction of an object. Proper use of constructors and destructors ensures efficient resource management.
- **RAII**: A best practice in C++ for resource management, ensuring resources are released when objects go out of scope.

Understanding constructors and destructors provides essential control over the initialization and cleanup of objects, an invaluable skill for managing resources and building robust, efficient applications. In the next chapter, we'll explore inheritance and polymorphism, which expand on the functionality of OOP by enabling classes to build upon each other.

CHAPTER 11: INHERITANCE AND POLYMORPHISM

Objective

This chapter introduces two essential OOP concepts: inheritance and polymorphism. Inheritance allows classes to inherit properties and behaviors from other classes, while polymorphism enables different classes to be treated as if they were instances of a common base class, leading to flexible and reusable code. By the end, readers will be able to create a base "Shape" class and derived classes for "Circle" and "Square" that demonstrate inheritance and polymorphism.

What is Inheritance?

Inheritance allows a new class (derived or child class) to inherit attributes and methods from an existing class (base or parent class). It promotes code reuse by enabling the child class to use and extend the behavior of the base class without duplicating code.

- **Syntax:**

cpp
```
class DerivedClass : access_specifier BaseClass {
    // Additional members and methods
};
```

  o **DerivedClass** inherits from BaseClass.

o **Access Specifier**: Determines which members of the base class are accessible in the derived class (usually public).

Types of Inheritance

1. **Single Inheritance**: A class inherits from a single base class.
2. **Multiple Inheritance**: A class inherits from multiple base classes (allowed in C++ but used with caution to avoid complexity).
3. **Multilevel Inheritance**: A class inherits from another derived class, creating a chain of inheritance.

What is Polymorphism?

Polymorphism allows objects of different classes to be treated as objects of a common base class. C++ achieves polymorphism through **virtual functions**, which enable a derived class to override a method from its base class.

There are two types of polymorphism:

1. **Compile-Time Polymorphism**: Achieved with function overloading and operator overloading.
2. **Runtime Polymorphism**: Achieved with virtual functions, allowing dynamic method resolution based on the actual type of the object.

Virtual Functions and Overriding

- A *virtual function* in a base class can be overridden in a derived class. This makes polymorphism possible because C++ determines which version of the function to call based on the type of the object at runtime.
- **Syntax**:

```cpp
virtual return_type function_name(parameters);
```

- **Pure Virtual Function**: A virtual function with no definition in the base class, making the class abstract. Derived classes must implement pure virtual functions.

```cpp
virtual void draw() = 0; // Pure virtual function
```

Example: Creating a Base "Shape" Class and Derived Classes "Circle" and "Square"

Let's create a Shape base class with a pure virtual function area() and two derived classes, Circle and Square, that implement this function.

1. **Base Class Definition**

```cpp
#include <iostream>
```

```cpp
#include <cmath> // For M_PI
using namespace std;

class Shape {
public:
    // Pure virtual function for calculating area
    virtual double area() const = 0;

    // Virtual function to display information
    virtual void display() const {
        cout << "This is a shape." << endl;
    }

    virtual ~Shape() {} // Virtual destructor for proper cleanup
};
```

- **Pure Virtual Function**: area() is a pure virtual function, making Shape an abstract class that cannot be instantiated. Derived classes must implement this function.
- **Virtual Destructor**: A virtual destructor ensures derived class destructors are called when a base class pointer deletes an object, preventing memory leaks.

2. **Derived Class: Circle**

cpp

```cpp
class Circle : public Shape {
private:
    double radius;

public:
    Circle(double r) : radius(r) {}

    // Override area() function
    double area() const override {
        return M_PI * radius * radius;
    }

    // Override display() function
    void display() const override {
        cout << "Circle with radius " << radius << " has area: " << area() << endl;
    }
};
```

- o **Constructor**: Initializes the radius of the circle.
- o **Overridden Methods**: area() calculates the area of the circle, and display() outputs details specific to the circle.

3. **Derived Class: Square**

cpp

Copy code

```
class Square : public Shape {
private:
    double side;

public:
    Square(double s) : side(s) {}

    // Override area() function
    double area() const override {
        return side * side;
    }

    // Override display() function
    void display() const override {
        cout << "Square with side " << side << " has area: " <<
area() << endl;
    }
};
```

- o **Constructor**: Initializes the side length of the square.
- o **Overridden Methods**: area() calculates the area of the square, and display() outputs details specific to the square.

4. **Using Inheritance and Polymorphism**

Now, let's create instances of Circle and Square and demonstrate polymorphism by calling their methods through a base class pointer.

cpp

```
int main() {
    // Create Circle and Square objects
    Shape* shape1 = new Circle(5.0);   // Circle with radius 5.0
    Shape* shape2 = new Square(4.0);   // Square with side 4.0

    // Display shape information
    shape1->display();
    shape2->display();

    // Clean up
    delete shape1;
    delete shape2;

    return 0;
}
```

5. **Expected Output**

csharp

Circle with radius 5 has area: 78.5398

Square with side 4 has area: 16

- o **Explanation**:
  - Both shape1 and shape2 are pointers to Shape objects, but they point to Circle and Square objects, respectively.
  - Due to polymorphism, the correct display() function for each derived class is called, even though the pointer is of type Shape*.

Detailed Explanation of OOP Concepts in the Shape Example

1. **Inheritance**:
   - o The Circle and Square classes inherit from Shape, reusing the base class's properties (like display() and area()) and adding unique implementations.
2. **Polymorphism**:
   - o The Shape* pointers allow objects of derived types to be treated as Shape objects, enabling dynamic behavior based on the actual object type (Circle or Square) at runtime.
3. **Virtual Functions and Overriding**:
   - o The display() and area() functions are overridden in the derived classes to provide specific behavior. The override keyword helps ensure these functions are correctly overridden.

4. **Abstract Class**:
   o The Shape class is abstract because it contains a pure virtual function area(). It cannot be instantiated, ensuring that only specific shapes (like Circle or Square) are created.

Benefits of Inheritance and Polymorphism

1. **Code Reusability**: Inheritance allows derived classes to reuse code from the base class, avoiding duplication.
2. **Flexibility and Scalability**: Polymorphism allows programs to use derived classes interchangeably through base class pointers, making it easy to add new shapes or behaviors without changing the existing code.
3. **Simplified Maintenance**: With polymorphism, derived classes handle their own implementations, reducing the need to modify code elsewhere.

Practice Exercises

1. **Animal Class with Derived Classes**: Create a base Animal class with a pure virtual function makeSound(). Implement derived classes like Dog and Cat, each with a unique makeSound() function. Use polymorphism to call makeSound() for different animal types.

2. **Employee Class with Subclasses**: Define a base Employee class with basic attributes (e.g., name and salary) and a virtual displayInfo() function. Create subclasses Manager and Developer, each with additional details. Demonstrate polymorphism by creating a list of employees.

3. **Vehicle Hierarchy**: Create a Vehicle base class with a virtual move() function. Implement derived classes like Car and Bicycle with specific move() implementations. Use polymorphism to simulate different vehicle movements.

- **Inheritance**: Allows a class to inherit properties and methods from another class, promoting code reuse.

- **Polymorphism**: Enables objects of derived classes to be treated as objects of the base class, providing flexibility and scalability in code.

- **Virtual Functions**: Allow derived classes to override methods, creating dynamic behavior based on the object's actual type.

- **Abstract Classes**: Classes with pure virtual functions that serve as blueprints for derived classes, enforcing specific behaviors.

Inheritance and polymorphism are powerful tools in OOP, allowing flexible and reusable code that models complex relationships between classes. In the next chapter, we'll explore operator

overloading, enabling classes to interact with operators like + or ==
in a way that's intuitive and meaningful for the object's context.

CHAPTER 12: OPERATOR OVERLOADING

Objective

In this chapter, we'll explore operator overloading, a feature in C++ that allows classes to redefine the behavior of operators (like +, -, *, etc.) for custom data types. This extends the functionality of classes, enabling objects to interact with operators in an intuitive way. By the end, readers will understand how to overload operators, demonstrated by overloading the + operator to add two complex numbers.

What is Operator Overloading?

Operator overloading allows C++ operators to be redefined to perform custom operations on user-defined types (classes and structs). It enhances the readability and usability of classes by allowing objects to use standard operators in a meaningful way.

- For example, instead of creating a method like `add()` to add two `Complex` objects, we can overload the + operator, making `complex1 + complex2` more intuitive.
- **Syntax**:

```cpp
Copy code
return_type operator symbol (parameters) {
    // Custom implementation
}
```

  - `return_type`: The return type of the overloaded operator.

- o **operator symbol**: The keyword `operator` followed by the symbol of the operator being overloaded.
- o **Parameters**: For binary operators (like + and -), the right-hand operand is passed as a parameter.

Rules for Operator Overloading

1. **Only Certain Operators Can Be Overloaded**: Most operators can be overloaded, but some cannot (e.g., . (member access), :: (scope resolution), and sizeof).

2. **Maintain Operator Semantics**: Overloaded operators should have intuitive behavior consistent with their original purpose.

3. **Overloading Syntax**: The keyword operator is followed by the symbol to be overloaded (e.g., `operator+` for +).

Example: Overloading the + Operator for Complex Numbers

A *complex number* has two parts: a real part and an imaginary part. We'll create a `Complex` class that overloads the + operator to add two complex numbers.

1. **Class Definition**

```cpp
Copy code
#include <iostream>
using namespace std;
```

```
class Complex {
private:
    double real;
    double imaginary;

public:
    // Constructor to initialize complex number
    Complex(double r = 0, double i = 0) :
real(r), imaginary(i) {}

    // Overload the + operator to add two
complex numbers
    Complex operator+(const Complex& other)
const {
        return Complex(real + other.real,
imaginary + other.imaginary);
    }

    // Method to display the complex number
    void display() const {
        cout << real << " + " << imaginary <<
"i" << endl;
    }
};
```

2. **Explanation**

   o **Constructor**: Complex(double r = 0, double i = 0) initializes the real and imaginary parts of the complex number. Default values of 0 allow for optional arguments.

   o **Overloaded + Operator**:

     ▪ Complex operator+(const Complex& other) const is a member function that overloads the + operator.

- It takes another Complex object as a parameter and returns a new Complex object with the sum of the real and imaginary parts.

  o **Display Method**: display() outputs the complex number in the format a + bi.

3. **Using the Overloaded + Operator**

```cpp
Copy code
int main() {
    Complex c1(3.0, 4.0);   // Complex number 3
+ 4i
    Complex c2(1.5, 2.5);   // Complex number
1.5 + 2.5i

    Complex c3 = c1 + c2;   // Using the
overloaded + operator

    cout << "c1: ";
    c1.display();
    cout << "c2: ";
    c2.display();
    cout << "c1 + c2: ";
    c3.display();

    return 0;
}
```

4. **Expected Output**

```go
Copy code
c1: 3 + 4i
c2: 1.5 + 2.5i
c1 + c2: 4.5 + 6.5i
```

   o **Explanation**: c3 = c1 + c2 uses the overloaded + operator to add c1 and c2. The result is stored in c3, which is displayed in the format `a + bi`.

Overloading Other Operators

Let's briefly look at overloading some other common operators.

1. **Overloading the - Operator**
   o This operator could be used to subtract one complex number from another.

```cpp
Copy code
Complex operator-(const Complex& other) const {
    return Complex(real - other.real, imaginary
- other.imaginary);
}
```

2. **Overloading the == Operator**
   o This operator could be used to compare two complex numbers for equality.

```cpp
Copy code
bool operator==(const Complex& other) const {
    return (real == other.real) && (imaginary
== other.imaginary);
}
```

3. **Overloading the << Operator (Stream Insertion)**
   o Overloading << allows us to use cout with Complex objects directly. This is done by defining the operator as a non-member function that takes an ostream object and a Complex object as parameters.

```cpp
Copy code
```

```
friend ostream& operator<<(ostream& os, const
Complex& c) {
    os << c.real << " + " << c.imaginary <<
"i";
    return os;
}
```

- **Usage**:

  ```
  cpp
  Copy code
  cout << c1 << endl; // Displays the
  complex number using the overloaded <<
  operator
  ```

Detailed Explanation of Operator Overloading Concepts in the Complex Example

1. **Binary Operators**:
   - $+$ is a binary operator that operates on two Complex objects. Overloading allows us to define how two complex numbers should be added together, making c1 + c2 intuitive.

2. **Member vs. Non-Member Functions**:
   - Most operators can be overloaded as member functions. However, operators like $<<$ and $>>$ are typically overloaded as non-member (friend) functions, as they require access to the left operand, which is usually a stream object (like cout).

3. **Return Type and Const Correctness**:
   - The $+$ operator returns a Complex object by value, allowing the result to be used directly.

    o The const keyword ensures that the function does not modify the object, which is essential for safe, predictable behavior.

Benefits of Operator Overloading

1. **Enhanced Readability**:
   - o Operator overloading allows code to be more intuitive. For instance, c1 + c2 is clearer and more concise than calling an add() function.

2. **Custom Functionality for User-Defined Types**:
   - o Operators can be given custom functionality that aligns with the specific needs of the class. In our example, + performs vector addition for complex numbers.

3. **Flexibility**:
   - o Operator overloading provides flexibility, enabling objects to work seamlessly with standard operators.

Practice Exercises

1. **Fraction Class with Overloaded Operators**: Create a Fraction class that represents fractions (e.g., 1/2, 3/4). Overload the +, -, *, and / operators to perform fraction arithmetic.

2. **Vector Class with Dot Product**: Write a Vector class with x, y, and z components. Overload the * operator to compute the dot product of two vectors.

3. **Matrix Class with Addition and Multiplication**: Create a Matrix class for 2x2 matrices and overload the + and * operators to perform matrix addition and multiplication.

- **Operator Overloading**: Allows operators to be customized for user-defined types, enabling natural, intuitive syntax for complex operations.

- **Binary Operators**: Common operators like +, -, and * can be overloaded as member functions, allowing operations between objects.

- **Stream Operators**: << and >> can be overloaded to integrate user-defined types with cin and cout, enhancing usability.

Operator overloading makes classes more intuitive and accessible by allowing familiar syntax for custom data types, which is especially useful for mathematical classes. In the next chapter, we'll explore file handling and streams, enabling programs to read from and write to external files, which is essential for data storage and management.

CHAPTER 13: WORKING WITH FILES AND STREAMS

Objective

This chapter covers file handling in C++, enabling programs to read from and write to external files. By working with files, programs can store and retrieve data, making it persistent across sessions. We'll explore file streams, reading, and writing techniques, along with a practical example that demonstrates reading from a text file and logging data.

Introduction to File Handling and Streams

C++ uses **streams** to handle data input and output. A stream is a flow of data that can be directed to various sources or destinations, like the console or files.

There are three main types of file streams:

1. `ifstream` (input file stream): Used to read data from files.
2. `ofstream` (output file stream): Used to write data to files.
3. `fstream` (file stream): Used for both reading and writing.

To use these file streams, include the `<fstream>` library.

Opening and Closing Files

1. **Opening a File**

    Files are opened by creating an `ifstream`, `ofstream`, or `fstream` object and specifying the file path. Files should be opened in the correct mode to avoid errors.

    o   **Syntax**:

        ```cpp
        Copy code
        ifstream inputFile("file.txt");     //
        Open a file for reading
        ofstream outputFile("output.txt"); //
        Open a file for writing
        ```

    o   Alternatively, you can use the `.open()` function:

        ```cpp
        Copy code
        ifstream inputFile;
        inputFile.open("file.txt");
        ```

2. **Checking if a File Opened Successfully**

    Before proceeding, always check if the file opened successfully:

    ```cpp
    Copy code
    if (!inputFile.is_open()) {
        cout << "Error: Could not open file." <<
    endl;
    }
    ```

3. **Closing a File**

After completing file operations, use `.close()` to release system resources.

```
cpp
Copy code
inputFile.close();
outputFile.close();
```

Reading from a File

To read data from a file, `ifstream` provides several methods:

1. **Reading Line by Line**: Use `getline()` to read lines from a file.

```
cpp
Copy code
string line;
while (getline(inputFile, line)) {
    cout << line << endl;
}
```

2. **Reading Word by Word**: Use the extraction operator (>>) to read word by word.

```
cpp
Copy code
string word;
while (inputFile >> word) {
    cout << word << " ";
}
```

3. **Reading Until EOF (End of File)**: Use the `.eof()` method in loops to check if the end of the file is reached.

```
cpp
Copy code
while (!inputFile.eof()) {
    inputFile >> word;
```

```
}
```

Writing to a File

To write data to a file, use `ofstream` or `fstream` with the `<<` operator.

1. **Basic Writing**:

```cpp
Copy code
ofstream outputFile("log.txt");
outputFile << "This is a log entry." << endl;
outputFile.close();
```

2. **Appending to a File**: Use the `ios::app` flag to append data to an existing file without overwriting it.

```cpp
Copy code
ofstream outputFile("log.txt", ios::app);
outputFile << "New log entry" << endl;
outputFile.close();
```

Example: Reading from and Logging Data to a Text File

Let's create a program that reads data from a file, processes it, and writes a summary to a log file. We'll assume the input file (`data.txt`) contains information on student scores, with each line formatted as follows:

```
Copy code
Alice 85
Bob 90
Charlie 78
```

Our program will read these lines, calculate the average score, and log the result to an output file (`log.txt`).

1. **Problem Statement**
   - Read each line from the file `data.txt`, extract names and scores, and calculate the average score.
   - Write the summary, including the average score, to `log.txt`.
2. **Code**

```cpp
Copy code
#include <iostream>
#include <fstream>
#include <string>
using namespace std;

int main() {
    ifstream inputFile("data.txt");
    ofstream outputFile("log.txt", ios::app);
// Open log file in append mode

    if (!inputFile.is_open() ||
!outputFile.is_open()) {
        cout << "Error: Could not open
file(s)." << endl;
        return 1;
    }

    string name;
    int score, totalScore = 0, count = 0;

    // Reading data and calculating total score
    while (inputFile >> name >> score) {
        totalScore += score;
        count++;
    }

    // Calculating average score
    double average = (count > 0) ?
static_cast<double>(totalScore) / count : 0;

    // Logging summary
    outputFile << "Number of students: " <<
count << endl;
```

```
        outputFile << "Average score: " << average
    << endl;
        outputFile << "--------------------------"
    << endl;

        cout << "Data has been logged to log.txt"
    << endl;

        // Closing files
        inputFile.close();
        outputFile.close();

        return 0;
    }
```

3. **Explanation**

   o **Opening Files**: `ifstream inputFile("data.txt")` opens the input file for reading, and `ofstream outputFile("log.txt", ios::app)` opens the output file in append mode.

   o **Reading Data**: The loop `while (inputFile >> name >> score)` reads each line, extracting the student's name and score. Each score is added to `totalScore`, and `count` tracks the number of entries.

   o **Calculating Average**: After reading all entries, the average score is calculated.

   o **Writing to the Log File**: The program logs the number of students and average score to `log.txt`.

○ **Closing Files**: Finally, both files are closed to release resources.

4. **Sample Files and Output**

○ **Input File (data.txt)**:

```
Copy code
Alice 85
Bob 90
Charlie 78
```

○ **Output File (log.txt) After Running the Program**:

```
markdown
Copy code
Number of students: 3
Average score: 84.3333
------------------------
```

Additional File Modes and Flags

C++ offers various flags to control file access and behavior:

1. `ios::in`: Open file for reading (default for `ifstream`).
2. `ios::out`: Open file for writing (default for `ofstream`). Overwrites existing content.
3. `ios::app`: Append to the end of the file without overwriting.
4. `ios::trunc`: Truncate the file if it exists (default behavior of `ios::out`).
5. `ios::binary`: Open file in binary mode (useful for non-text files).

File Handling Best Practices

1. **Always Check If a File Opened Successfully**:
   - Ensure the file opened correctly before proceeding with reading or writing.
2. **Close Files After Use**:
   - Closing files frees system resources and avoids potential data corruption.

3. **Use Append Mode for Logging**:
   - Opening a file in append mode (ios::app) prevents overwriting existing data, which is useful for logging.

4. **Error Handling**:
   - Use error handling to manage scenarios where files may be missing or unreadable, providing user-friendly messages.

Practice Exercises

1. **Copy File Content**: Write a program that reads data from one file and writes it to another.
2. **Count Words in a File**: Create a program that reads a text file and counts the total number of words.
3. **Store and Retrieve Contacts**: Write a program to store contact names and phone numbers in a file, and then retrieve and display them.

- **File Streams**: ifstream, ofstream, and fstream allow for reading from and writing to files in C++.

- **File Operations**: Reading with getline() and >>, writing with <<, and opening files in different modes are essential for file handling.

- **Logging and Appending**: Using append mode allows for logging data without overwriting existing content.

- **Error Checking**: Checking if files opened successfully is crucial for reliable file handling.

File handling is essential for data persistence, enabling applications to read and store information across sessions. In the next chapter, we'll delve into exception handling, which will help manage errors gracefully and keep programs running smoothly in the face of unexpected issues.

CHAPTER 14: EXCEPTION HANDLING AND DEBUGGING

Objective

This chapter introduces error handling using try and catch blocks, as well as essential debugging techniques. Exception handling allows programs to handle unexpected situations gracefully, improving their robustness and reliability. By the end of this chapter, readers will understand how to use exception handling to validate user input and use debugging techniques to identify and fix issues in code.

What is Exception Handling?

Exception handling is a mechanism to handle runtime errors, or *exceptions*, in a controlled way. In C++, exceptions provide a way to transfer control from the point of error to a block of code designed to handle that error, allowing the program to recover or terminate gracefully.

1. **Exceptions**: An *exception* is an error or unexpected condition that occurs during program execution.

2. **try Block**: Code that may throw an exception is placed inside a try block.

3. **catch Block**: A catch block is used to handle exceptions thrown by the try block.

- **Syntax**:

cpp

```
try {
    // Code that may throw an exception
} catch (exception_type e) {
    // Code to handle the exception
}
```

Throwing and Catching Exceptions

1. **Throwing Exceptions**

   When an error occurs, an exception can be ***thrown*** using the throw keyword. The thrown exception can be a value or an object, which is then passed to the catch block.

   cpp

   Copy code

   ```
   throw "Error: Invalid input";
   ```

2. **Catching Exceptions**

   The catch block catches thrown exceptions. It should match the type of the exception being thrown, which can be a built-in type (like int or string) or a custom exception class.

   cpp

   Copy code

   ```
   try {
   ```

```cpp
    throw "An error occurred";
} catch (const char* errorMessage) {
    cout << errorMessage << endl;
}
```

Example: Implementing Exception Handling for User Input Validation

Let's create a program that takes user input, ensuring that it is a valid number and within a specific range. If the user enters invalid input, the program will throw and catch exceptions to handle the error.

1. **Problem Statement**
   - Prompt the user to enter a positive integer less than 100.
   - If the user enters a non-integer or an out-of-range value, throw an exception.
   - Catch the exception and display an error message, allowing the user to re-enter a valid value.
2. **Code**

```cpp
cpp
#include <iostream>
#include <stdexcept> // For standard exception classes
using namespace std;

int getUserInput() {
```

```cpp
    int number;
    cout << "Enter a positive integer less than 100: ";

    try {
        if (!(cin >> number)) { // Check for non-integer input
            throw invalid_argument("Input is not an integer.");
        }
        if (number < 0 || number >= 100) { // Check range
            throw out_of_range("Number is out of valid range
(0-99).");
        }
    } catch (const invalid_argument& e) {
        cin.clear(); // Clear the error state of cin
        cin.ignore(10000, '\n'); // Discard invalid input
        cout << "Error: " << e.what() << endl;
        return getUserInput(); // Prompt the user again
    } catch (const out_of_range& e) {
        cout << "Error: " << e.what() << endl;
        return getUserInput(); // Prompt the user again
    }

    return number; // Return valid input
}

int main() {
```

```cpp
    int validInput = getUserInput();
    cout << "You entered: " << validInput << endl;
    return 0;
}
```

3. **Explanation**

   o **getUserInput Function**: Prompts the user for an integer input. If the input fails or is out of range, exceptions are thrown.

   - **Invalid Argument Exception**: throw invalid_argument("Input is not an integer.") is thrown if the input is non-numeric.

   - **Out of Range Exception**: throw out_of_range("Number is out of valid range (0-99).") is thrown if the input is outside the specified range.

   o **Catch Blocks**: Handle each type of exception with invalid_argument and out_of_range, displaying an error message and prompting the user to enter the input again.

4. **Sample Output**

vbnet

Enter a positive integer less than 100: hello

Error: Input is not an integer.

Common Exception Types

C++ provides several built-in exception types in the <stdexcept> library:

1. **invalid_argument**: Thrown when an invalid argument is provided to a function.
2. **out_of_range**: Thrown when a value is outside the valid range.
3. **runtime_error**: Used for general runtime errors.
4. **overflow_error** and **underflow_error**: Thrown for arithmetic overflows and underflows.

Custom Exceptions

In addition to built-in exceptions, you can define custom exceptions by creating a class that inherits from std::exception.

cpp

```cpp
class CustomException : public exception {
public:
    const char* what() const noexcept override {
        return "Custom exception occurred!";
    }
};
```

- **Usage**:

    cpp

throw CustomException();

Debugging Techniques

1. **Using Print Statements**
   o Adding cout statements to display variable values and program flow is one of the simplest debugging techniques. It helps track down logical errors and see how data changes.

2. **Using a Debugger**
   o Modern IDEs like Visual Studio, CLion, and Code::Blocks offer integrated debuggers that allow you to set breakpoints, step through code, and inspect variable values in real-time.

3. **Breakpoints and Step Execution**
   o **Breakpoints**: Pauses execution at specific points in the code to inspect the state.
   o **Step Execution**: Allows you to execute code line by line (Step Over, Step Into, Step Out), making it easier to isolate and diagnose issues.

4. **Examining Call Stacks**
   o The *call stack* shows the sequence of function calls that led to the current point in the program. It's helpful for tracking the flow of recursive functions or deeply nested calls.

5. **Watching Variables**

o Debuggers allow you to *watch* variables, displaying their values as you step through the code. This helps you see how data changes over time.

Benefits of Exception Handling and Debugging

1. **Error Resilience**: Exception handling helps applications continue running or terminate gracefully even when unexpected errors occur.
2. **Improved Code Reliability**: By handling potential errors, you can prevent crashes and manage unexpected behavior more effectively.
3. **Easier Problem Diagnosis**: Debugging tools simplify the identification of logic errors and bugs, reducing development time and improving code quality.

Practice Exercises

1. **Division with Exception Handling**: Create a program that prompts the user for two integers and divides them. Use exception handling to prevent division by zero and prompt the user to enter a new value if zero is entered.
2. **File Handling with Exceptions**: Write a program that opens a file for reading and handles exceptions if the file doesn't exist or fails to open.

3. **Calculator with Custom Exceptions**: Develop a calculator that performs basic arithmetic operations. Use custom exceptions to handle invalid operations and out-of-range inputs.

- **Exception Handling**: Allows programs to handle runtime errors in a controlled way, preventing abrupt crashes and providing users with meaningful error messages.
- **try, catch, and throw**: The basic constructs of exception handling in C++ for defining, throwing, and handling exceptions.
- **Debugging Techniques**: Tools like breakpoints, variable watching, and step execution simplify finding and fixing bugs in code.

Exception handling and debugging are essential skills for writing robust, error-resistant programs. Together, they allow you to manage errors gracefully, identify problems, and ensure that your code runs smoothly under various conditions. In the next chapter, we'll explore templates and generic programming, which will help create functions and classes that work with any data type, enhancing code reusability and flexibility.

CHAPTER 15: TEMPLATES AND GENERIC PROGRAMMING

Objective

This chapter introduces templates and generic programming in C++, which allow you to write reusable code that can work with various data types. Templates enable functions and classes to operate on different types without rewriting code for each type. By the end, readers will be able to create a generic function to sort arrays of different data types.

What are Templates?

Templates in C++ allow you to create functions and classes that work with any data type. Instead of specifying a specific data type, a placeholder type is used, which is replaced by an actual data type when the function or class is used.

There are two main types of templates:

1. **Function Templates**: Enable functions to operate on any data type.
2. **Class Templates**: Enable classes to work with any data type.

Function Templates

A *function template* is a blueprint for creating functions with different data types. Instead of defining multiple functions (like int add(int, int) and float add(float, float)), you define a single template that works with any type.

- **Syntax**:

cpp
Copy code
template <typename T>
return_type function_name(parameters) {
    // Function implementation
}

  - o template <typename T>: Declares a template with a type parameter T. You can use any name in place of T, but T (for Type) is common.
  - o **T**: Acts as a placeholder for the data type and will be replaced by the actual type when the function is called.

Example: Function Template for Finding Maximum

This function template returns the maximum of two values, regardless of their type.

cpp
Copy code
#include <iostream>
using namespace std;

```
template <typename T>
T getMax(T a, T b) {
    return (a > b) ? a : b;
}

int main() {
    cout << "Max of 10 and 20: " << getMax(10, 20) << endl;      // Works with int
    cout << "Max of 5.5 and 3.3: " << getMax(5.5, 3.3) << endl;   // Works with double
    cout << "Max of 'a' and 'z': " << getMax('a', 'z') << endl;   // Works with char

    return 0;
}
```

- **Explanation**: getMax is a template function that works with any type, such as int, double, or char. When calling getMax(10, 20), T is automatically deduced as int.

Class Templates

A *class template* allows you to define a class that can handle any data type. This is useful for creating generic data structures, like stacks, queues, and linked lists, without specifying a specific data type.

147

- **Syntax**:

```cpp
template <typename T>
class ClassName {
    // Use T as the data type within the class
};
```

Example: Class Template for a Simple Pair

This example defines a class Pair that holds two values of the same type.

```cpp
#include <iostream>
using namespace std;

template <typename T>
class Pair {
private:
    T first;
    T second;

public:
    Pair(T a, T b) : first(a), second(b) {}

    T getFirst() const { return first; }
```

```
    T getSecond() const { return second; }
};
```

```
int main() {
    Pair<int> intPair(10, 20);        // Pair of integers
    Pair<string> stringPair("Hello", "World"); // Pair of strings

    cout << "Integer Pair: " << intPair.getFirst() << ", " <<
intPair.getSecond() << endl;
    cout << "String Pair: " << stringPair.getFirst() << ", " <<
stringPair.getSecond() << endl;

    return 0;
}
```

- **Explanation**: The Pair class template works with any data type, storing two values of that type. We create an int pair and a string pair, demonstrating the flexibility of class templates.

Example: Generic Function to Sort Arrays of Different Data Types

Now, let's create a generic function template to sort an array. This function will work for arrays of any data type, whether int, double, char, etc.

1. **Problem Statement**

    o   Write a template function sortArray that takes an array and its size as arguments, then sorts the array in ascending order.

2. **Code**

```cpp
#include <iostream>
using namespace std;

template <typename T>
void sortArray(T arr[], int size) {
    for (int i = 0; i < size - 1; i++) {
        for (int j = i + 1; j < size; j++) {
            if (arr[i] > arr[j]) {
                // Swap elements
                T temp = arr[i];
                arr[i] = arr[j];
                arr[j] = temp;
            }
        }
    }
}
```

```
template <typename T>
void printArray(T arr[], int size) {
  for (int i = 0; i < size; i++) {
    cout << arr[i] << " ";
  }
  cout << endl;
}

int main() {
  int intArray[] = {5, 2, 9, 1, 5, 6};
  double doubleArray[] = {3.5, 2.1, 9.6, 1.2, 5.5};

  int intSize = sizeof(intArray) / sizeof(intArray[0]);
  int doubleSize = sizeof(doubleArray) / sizeof(doubleArray[0]);

  // Sort and print integer array
  cout << "Original int array: ";
  printArray(intArray, intSize);
  sortArray(intArray, intSize);
  cout << "Sorted int array: ";
  printArray(intArray, intSize);

  // Sort and print double array
  cout << "Original double array: ";
```

```
printArray(doubleArray, doubleSize);
sortArray(doubleArray, doubleSize);
cout << "Sorted double array: ";
printArray(doubleArray, doubleSize);

return 0;
}
```

3. **Explanation**

   o **sortArray Template**: The sortArray function is a template function that works with any data type T. It sorts an array of any type in ascending order using a simple bubble sort algorithm.

   o **printArray Template**: The printArray function is a template for displaying arrays of any type.

   o **Using sortArray**: We call sortArray for both an int array and a double array, showing that it works with multiple types.

4. **Sample Output**

```
c
Original int array: 5 2 9 1 5 6
Sorted int array: 1 2 5 5 6 9
Original double array: 3.5 2.1 9.6 1.2 5.5
Sorted double array: 1.2 2.1 3.5 5.5 9.6
```

Advantages of Templates

1. **Code Reusability**: Templates reduce code duplication by allowing functions and classes to operate on any data type, making code more reusable and maintainable.

2. **Type Safety**: Unlike macros or casting, templates maintain type safety by enforcing type checks at compile time.

3. **Generic Algorithms**: Templates enable the creation of generic algorithms and data structures that work with any type (e.g., sorting algorithms, data structures like stacks and queues).

Template Specialization

In some cases, you may want to customize the behavior of a template for a specific data type. ***Template specialization*** allows you to define a special implementation of a template for a specific type.

- **Syntax**:

```cpp
template <>
class ClassName<specialized_type> {
    // Specialized implementation for the specific type
};
```

Example: Specialized Template for printArray with char Type

For char arrays, we may want to print them as strings rather than individual characters. Here's how you could specialize printArray for char arrays.

```cpp
template <>
void printArray(char arr[], int size) {
    cout << arr << endl; // Print as a string
}
```

Practice Exercises

1. **Generic Calculator**: Create a function template add that takes two values of any type and returns their sum. Test it with int, float, and double types.

2. **Queue Class Template**: Implement a Queue class template with methods for enqueuing, dequeuing, and checking if the queue is empty. Use it for int and string data types.

3. **Min and Max Finder**: Write a template function findMinMax that takes an array and its size, then returns the minimum and maximum values in the array. Test it with int and double arrays.

- **Templates**: Allow functions and classes to work with any data type, making code reusable and flexible.

- **Function Templates**: Define functions that operate on any data type.

- **Class Templates**: Enable classes to handle multiple data types, useful for generic data structures.

- **Template Specialization**: Allows customization of a template for specific data types when unique behavior is required.

Templates and generic programming add powerful flexibility and reusability to C++, enabling code to work with a wide range of types without redundancy. In the next chapter, we'll delve into the Standard Template Library (STL), which leverages templates to provide a collection of highly optimized, ready-to-use data structures and algorithms.

Chapter 16: The Standard Template Library (STL)

Objective

This chapter introduces the Standard Template Library (STL), a powerful C++ library of template-based classes and functions that provide common data structures (containers) and algorithms. By using STL, developers can create efficient and readable code quickly. We'll focus on essential containers like vector, list, and map, along with some core algorithms. By the end, readers will understand how to use a vector to store and manage a list of users.

What is the Standard Template Library (STL)?

The STL is a collection of template-based data structures and algorithms. It allows you to efficiently manage and manipulate data using well-optimized, reusable components. The STL is divided into three main components:

1. **Containers**: Data structures that store collections of elements, such as vector, list, and map.
2. **Algorithms**: Functions that perform operations on data stored in containers, like sort, find, and accumulate.
3. **Iterators**: Objects that provide a way to traverse elements in containers, similar to pointers.

Containers

Containers are data structures that hold and organize data. Some of the most commonly used STL containers include:

1. **vector**: A dynamic array that can grow in size.
2. **list**: A doubly-linked list that allows efficient insertion and deletion at any position.
3. **map**: A collection of key-value pairs where each key is unique, often used for associative data storage.

Using vector

A vector is a dynamic array that can resize itself automatically when new elements are added. It provides fast access to elements and is often the go-to container when you need an array-like structure with dynamic resizing.

- **Syntax**:

```cpp
Copy code
#include <vector>
vector<data_type> vector_name;
```

1. **Basic Operations with vector**
    - **Adding Elements**: Use .push_back() to add elements to the end of a vector.

cpp

```cpp
vector<int> numbers;
numbers.push_back(10);
numbers.push_back(20);
```

o **Accessing Elements**: Use indexing ([]) or .at().

cpp

```cpp
cout << numbers[0];  // Accesses the first element
```

o **Removing Elements**: Use .pop_back() to remove the last element.

cpp

```cpp
numbers.pop_back();
```

o **Size and Capacity**: .size() returns the number of elements, and .capacity() returns the total allocated storage.

cpp

```cpp
cout << "Size: " << numbers.size() << endl;
cout << "Capacity: " << numbers.capacity() << endl;
```

Example: Using a Vector to Manage a List of Users

Let's create a program that uses a vector to store and manage a list of users. Each user will have a name, and the program will allow adding, displaying, and removing users.

1. **Problem Statement**
   - o Define a User structure with a name attribute.
   - o Use a vector to store a list of User objects.
   - o Implement functions to add users, display all users, and remove a user by name.

2. **Code**

```cpp
cpp
#include <iostream>
#include <vector>
#include <string>
using namespace std;

// Define a User structure
struct User {
    string name;
};

// Function to add a user
void addUser(vector<User>& users, const string& name) {
    users.push_back(User{name});
    cout << "User " << name << " added." << endl;
}

// Function to display all users
```

```cpp
void displayUsers(const vector<User>& users) {
  if (users.empty()) {
    cout << "No users to display." << endl;
  } else {
    cout << "List of Users:" << endl;
    for (const auto& user : users) {
      cout << "- " << user.name << endl;
    }
  }
}


// Function to remove a user by name
void removeUser(vector<User>& users, const string& name) {
  auto it = find_if(users.begin(), users.end(), [&name](const User& user) {
    return user.name == name;
  });

  if (it != users.end()) {
    users.erase(it);
    cout << "User " << name << " removed." << endl;
  } else {
    cout << "User " << name << " not found." << endl;
  }
```

```
}

int main() {
    vector<User> users;
    addUser(users, "Alice");
    addUser(users, "Bob");
    addUser(users, "Charlie");

    displayUsers(users);

    removeUser(users, "Bob");

    displayUsers(users);

    return 0;
}
```

3. **Explanation**

- **User Structure**: The User structure contains a name attribute to represent a user.
- **Vector of Users**: vector<User> users; stores multiple User objects.
- **addUser Function**: Adds a new user to the vector.
- **displayUsers Function**: Iterates through the vector to display all users.

o **removeUser Function**: Finds and removes a user by name, using find_if and a lambda function for searching.

4. **Expected Output**

diff

User Alice added.

User Bob added.

User Charlie added.

List of Users:

- Alice

- Bob

- Charlie

User Bob removed.

List of Users:

- Alice

- Charlie

Other STL Containers

1. **list**: A doubly-linked list that allows efficient insertions and deletions.

o **Syntax**:

```cpp
#include <list>
list<int> numbers;
```

- o **Basic Operations**:
  - ▪ .push_back() and .push_front() add elements to the end and beginning.
  - ▪ .pop_back() and .pop_front() remove elements from the end and beginning.
2. **map**: An associative container that stores key-value pairs, where each key is unique.
   - o **Syntax**:

cpp
Copy code
#include <map>
map<string, int> phonebook;

   - o **Basic Operations**:
     - ▪ **Adding Elements**: phonebook["Alice"] = 123456789;
     - ▪ **Accessing Elements**: cout << phonebook["Alice"];
     - ▪ **Removing Elements**: phonebook.erase("Alice");

STL Algorithms

The STL provides a range of algorithms that work with containers, such as sort, find, and accumulate.

1. **sort**: Sorts elements in a container. Requires iterators for the beginning and end of the range to be sorted.

cpp

Copy code

```cpp
vector<int> numbers = {4, 2, 3, 1, 5};
sort(numbers.begin(), numbers.end());
```

2. **find**: Searches for an element in a container and returns an iterator to it if found.

cpp

Copy code

```cpp
auto it = find(numbers.begin(), numbers.end(), 3);
if (it != numbers.end()) {
    cout << "Element found!" << endl;
}
```

3. **accumulate**: Calculates the sum of elements in a range.

cpp

Copy code

```cpp
#include <numeric>
int sum = accumulate(numbers.begin(), numbers.end(), 0);
```

Benefits of Using the STL

1. **Efficiency**: STL containers and algorithms are optimized for performance.
2. **Code Reusability**: STL offers generic implementations of data structures and algorithms that work for multiple data types.
3. **Reduced Complexity**: STL makes it easy to implement complex tasks with concise, readable code.

Practice Exercises

1. **Student Grade Manager**: Use a vector to store student names and grades. Implement functions to add, display, and find students by name.
2. **Contact Book with Map**: Use a map to store names and phone numbers. Allow the user to add, search, and delete contacts.
3. **Shopping List with List**: Use a list to manage a shopping list. Implement functions to add, remove, and display items in the list.

- **STL**: The Standard Template Library provides reusable data structures (containers) and algorithms.
- **Containers**: Common containers include vector, list, and map, each suited to specific use cases.

- **Algorithms**: Functions like sort, find, and accumulate enable easy data manipulation within containers.
- **Iterators**: Provide a way to traverse and manipulate elements within containers.

The STL is an essential part of C++ programming, offering efficient, flexible, and reusable tools for managing and processing data. In the next chapter, we'll cover smart pointers, which handle memory management automatically, reducing the chances of memory leaks and simplifying resource handling.

HAPTER 17: ADVANCED DATA STRUCTURES

Objective

This chapter delves into more advanced data structures, specifically linked lists, stacks, and queues. These structures allow for efficient data organization, manipulation, and management in scenarios where dynamic data handling is necessary. By the end, readers will be able to implement a stack using a linked list.

Introduction to Linked Lists, Stacks, and Queues

1. **Linked List**: A collection of nodes where each node contains data and a pointer to the next node. It's dynamic and allows efficient insertions and deletions.

2. **Stack**: A last-in, first-out (LIFO) data structure, where the last element added is the first to be removed. Operations are restricted to the top of the stack.

3. **Queue**: A first-in, first-out (FIFO) data structure, where the first element added is the first to be removed. Operations are restricted to the front and back.

Linked Lists

A *linked list* is a series of connected nodes, where each node holds data and a reference (or pointer) to the next node in the sequence.

1. **Node Structure**

Each node in a linked list typically consists of:

- o **Data**: The value stored in the node.
- o **Pointer**: A reference to the next node.

```cpp
struct Node {
    int data;
    Node* next;
    Node(int val) : data(val), next(nullptr) {}
};
```

2. **Types of Linked Lists**
   - o **Singly Linked List**: Each node points to the next node in the sequence.
   - o **Doubly Linked List**: Each node points to both the next and previous nodes.
   - o **Circular Linked List**: The last node points back to the first node, creating a circular structure.

3. **Basic Operations on Linked Lists**
   - o **Insertion**: Adding a node at the beginning, end, or at a specific position.
   - o **Deletion**: Removing a node from the beginning, end, or a specific position.

    o   **Traversal**: Moving through each node to access data.

Stack

A *stack* is a LIFO data structure, meaning that the last element added to the stack is the first to be removed. It's useful for tasks where data needs to be processed in reverse order, such as function call management, expression evaluation, and undo operations.

1. **Stack Operations**
   - o **Push**: Add an element to the top of the stack.
   - o **Pop**: Remove the top element from the stack.
   - o **Peek (Top)**: Retrieve the top element without removing it.
   - o **isEmpty**: Check if the stack is empty.
2. **Implementing a Stack Using a Linked List**

   By implementing a stack with a linked list, we can dynamically manage data without needing a predefined size, unlike array-based stacks.

Example: Implementing a Stack Using a Linked List

Let's create a simple stack that uses a linked list. This stack will support push, pop, peek, and isEmpty operations.

1. **Problem Statement**
   - o Implement a stack using a singly linked list.

    o   Define methods for pushing, popping, peeking, and checking if the stack is empty.

2. **Code**

```cpp
cpp
#include <iostream>
using namespace std;

// Node structure for linked list
struct Node {
    int data;
    Node* next;
    Node(int val) : data(val), next(nullptr) {}
};

// Stack class using linked list
class Stack {
private:
    Node* top; // Points to the top of the stack

public:
    // Constructor
    Stack() : top(nullptr) {}

    // Push method
```

```cpp
void push(int value) {
    Node* newNode = new Node(value);
    newNode->next = top;
    top = newNode;
    cout << "Pushed " << value << " onto the stack." <<
endl;
}

// Pop method
void pop() {
    if (isEmpty()) {
        cout << "Stack is empty. Nothing to pop." << endl;
        return;
    }
    Node* temp = top;
    top = top->next;
    cout << "Popped " << temp->data << " from the stack."
<< endl;
    delete temp;
}

// Peek method
int peek() const {
    if (isEmpty()) {
        cout << "Stack is empty. No top element." << endl;
```

```cpp
        return -1; // Using -1 as an error code
    }
    return top->data;
}

// isEmpty method
bool isEmpty() const {
    return top == nullptr;
}

// Destructor to free memory
~Stack() {
    while (!isEmpty()) {
        pop();
    }
}
};

int main() {
    Stack stack;

    stack.push(10);
    stack.push(20);
    stack.push(30);
```

```
cout << "Top element is: " << stack.peek() << endl;

stack.pop();
stack.pop();

cout << "Top element after popping is: " << stack.peek()
<< endl;

stack.pop();
stack.pop(); // Attempt to pop from empty stack

return 0;
}
```

3. **Explanation**

   o **Node Structure**: Each Node represents an element in the stack, with data and a pointer to the next node.

   o **Stack Class**:

     ▪ **Push**: Adds a new node at the top by creating a new Node, setting its next pointer to the current top, and updating top to the new node.

     ▪ **Pop**: Removes the top node by updating top to point to the next node and deleting the removed node.

- **Peek**: Returns the data of the top node without modifying the stack.

- **isEmpty**: Checks if the top pointer is nullptr, indicating an empty stack.

  o **Destructor**: Cleans up all nodes when the stack is destroyed, preventing memory leaks.

4. **Expected Output**

vbnet

Copy code

Pushed 10 onto the stack.

Pushed 20 onto the stack.

Pushed 30 onto the stack.

Top element is: 30

Popped 30 from the stack.

Popped 20 from the stack.

Top element after popping is: 10

Popped 10 from the stack.

Stack is empty. Nothing to pop.

Queue

A *queue* is a FIFO data structure, meaning that the first element added to the queue is the first to be removed. Queues are ideal for handling tasks where order matters, like scheduling processes, managing print jobs, and handling tasks in real-time systems.

1. **Queue Operations**

   o **Enqueue**: Add an element to the end of the queue.

   o **Dequeue**: Remove the element from the front of the queue.

   o **Front**: Retrieve the element at the front without removing it.

   o **isEmpty**: Check if the queue is empty.

2. **Implementing a Queue Using a Linked List**

   In a linked list-based queue, each node represents an element, and the queue keeps track of the front and rear nodes for efficient enqueue and dequeue operations.

Benefits of Using Advanced Data Structures

1. **Dynamic Data Management**: Linked lists allow dynamic data storage, unlike arrays with fixed sizes.

2. **Efficient Element Management**: Stacks and queues manage elements based on access order, simplifying tasks like undo functions, task scheduling, and request handling.

3. **Flexibility**: Linked lists provide greater flexibility for insertions and deletions, making them useful in applications requiring frequent modifications.

Practice Exercises

1. **Linked List Implementation**: Implement a singly linked list with functions to add, delete, and display nodes.
2. **Queue Implementation Using Linked List**: Implement a queue using a linked list, with enqueue, dequeue, front, and isEmpty operations.
3. **Browser Back Button Simulation**: Use a stack to implement a simple browser back button function, allowing users to go back to previous pages.

- **Linked Lists**: Dynamic data structures that allow efficient insertions and deletions, useful for implementing stacks and queues.
- **Stack**: A LIFO data structure for scenarios requiring reverse processing order, like undo functions.
- **Queue**: A FIFO data structure ideal for order-dependent tasks, such as task scheduling.
- **Memory Management**: Linked list-based structures avoid fixed memory constraints, unlike arrays, providing flexibility in data handling.

Mastering these advanced data structures helps in building efficient, flexible, and powerful programs. In the next chapter, we'll explore smart pointers, which simplify memory management by automatically handling resource allocation and deallocation, reducing the risk of memory leaks in complex programs.

CHAPTER 18: MULTITHREADING AND CONCURRENCY

Objective

This chapter introduces multithreading in C++, a technique that allows a program to perform multiple tasks simultaneously. We'll discuss how to create and manage threads, and explore concurrency control mechanisms like mutexes to prevent data races. By the end, readers will understand how to use multiple threads to calculate the sum of large datasets, demonstrating the basics of concurrent programming.

What is Multithreading?

Multithreading is a programming approach where multiple threads execute independently but share the same memory space. This enables tasks to be performed in parallel, making programs faster and more efficient on multicore processors.

1. **Thread**: The smallest unit of execution within a process. A process can have multiple threads running in parallel.

2. **Concurrency**: The ability to execute multiple tasks simultaneously, increasing a program's efficiency and responsiveness.

3. **Parallelism**: The simultaneous execution of tasks on multiple cores, improving performance for tasks that can be processed concurrently.

Creating and Managing Threads in C++

The <thread> library in C++ provides the functionality to create and manage threads.

1. **Creating a Thread**
   o To create a thread, initialize a std::thread object with a function to be executed. The thread starts running the function as soon as it's created.

   cpp
   ```
   #include <thread>

   void task() {
       // Task to be executed by the thread
   }

   int main() {
       std::thread t(task); // Create a thread and run task()
       t.join();       // Wait for thread t to complete
       return 0;
   }
   ```

2. **Joining Threads**

   o join(): The join method blocks the main thread until the thread completes its task.

   o detach(): Separates the thread from the main thread, allowing it to run independently. However, detached threads can't be joined later.

3. **Passing Arguments to Threads**

   o Arguments can be passed to a thread function by passing them to the std::thread constructor.

   cpp
   ```cpp
   void task(int n) {
       // Task that takes an integer argument
   }

   int main() {
       std::thread t(task, 5); // Pass 5 as an argument to task
       t.join();
       return 0;
   }
   ```

Concurrency Control with Mutexes

When multiple threads access shared resources, they can interfere with each other, causing issues like ***data races***. Mutexes (mutual exclusion locks) help manage this by allowing only one thread at a time to access a critical section.

1. **Using a Mutex**

   o A std::mutex can be locked before accessing a shared resource and unlocked after access is complete.

   ```cpp
   #include <mutex>

   std::mutex mtx;

   void safeTask() {
       mtx.lock();      // Lock the mutex
       // Critical section
       mtx.unlock();    // Unlock the mutex
   }
   ```

2. **Using std::lock_guard for Automatic Locking and Unlocking**

   o std::lock_guard automatically locks a mutex when it's created and unlocks it when it goes out of scope, ensuring the mutex is properly released.

   ```cpp
   ```

```cpp
void safeTask() {
    std::lock_guard<std::mutex> lock(mtx);
    // Critical section, mutex is automatically
    unlocked when lock goes out of scope
}
```

Example: Calculating the Sum of Large Datasets Using Multiple Threads

Let's create a program that calculates the sum of a large dataset by dividing it into parts and using multiple threads to calculate the sum of each part in parallel.

1. **Problem Statement**
   o Create an array with a large number of elements.
   o Divide the array into chunks, assigning each chunk to a separate thread for summing.
   o Use a mutex to safely add each thread's partial sum to the total sum.

2. **Code**

```cpp
cpp
#include <iostream>
#include <vector>
#include <thread>
#include <numeric> // For std::accumulate
#include <mutex>
```

```cpp
std::mutex mtx; // Mutex for protecting shared data
long long totalSum = 0; // Shared variable for total sum

// Function to calculate the sum of a portion of the array
void partialSum(const std::vector<int>& arr, int start, int
end) {
    long long partialSum = std::accumulate(arr.begin() +
start, arr.begin() + end, 0LL);

    // Lock the mutex before modifying the shared variable
    std::lock_guard<std::mutex> lock(mtx);
    totalSum += partialSum;
}

int main() {
    // Create a large array of integers
    const int dataSize = 1000000;
    std::vector<int> data(dataSize, 1); // Initialize with 1 for
simplicity

    // Number of threads
    const int numThreads = 4;
    std::vector<std::thread> threads;
    int chunkSize = dataSize / numThreads;
```

```
// Create threads to calculate the partial sum for each
chunk
    for (int i = 0; i < numThreads; ++i) {
        int start = i * chunkSize;
        int end = (i == numThreads - 1) ? dataSize : start +
chunkSize;
        threads.push_back(std::thread(partialSum,
std::ref(data), start, end));
    }

    // Join all threads
    for (auto& t : threads) {
        t.join();
    }

    // Display the total sum
    std::cout << "Total Sum: " << totalSum << std::endl;

    return 0;
}
```

3. **Explanation**

   o **Array Initialization**: A large vector data is initialized with 1 for simplicity.

- o **Partial Sum Calculation**: The partialSum function takes a portion of the array, calculates its sum, and then locks the mutex to add the result to totalSum.
- o **Dividing Work Among Threads**: The array is divided into numThreads chunks, each handled by a separate thread.
- o **Joining Threads**: All threads are joined to ensure they complete before displaying the total sum.
- o **Concurrency Control**: std::lock_guard is used to safely modify totalSum without data races.

4. **Expected Output**

mathematica

Copy code

Total Sum: 1000000

- o **Explanation**: Since the array contains 1,000,000 elements, each initialized to 1, the total sum is 1,000,000.

Thread Safety and Synchronization

1. **Data Races**: Occur when two or more threads access the same resource simultaneously, and at least one of the accesses is a write.

2. **Mutexes**: Ensure only one thread can access a critical section at a time, preventing data races.

3. **Condition Variables**: Allow threads to wait for specific conditions to be met, enabling thread synchronization.

Benefits of Multithreading

1. **Improved Performance**: Multithreading can take advantage of multiple CPU cores, increasing program efficiency for tasks that can be performed concurrently.

2. **Responsive Applications**: Programs with multiple threads can remain responsive while performing background tasks, such as loading resources or handling user input.

3. **Efficient Resource Utilization**: Parallelizing tasks helps in fully utilizing CPU resources, especially on modern multicore processors.

Practice Exercises

1. **Parallel Array Sum**: Modify the example program to divide the dataset into a user-specified number of chunks, allowing flexible division of work across threads.

2. **Prime Number Counter**: Create a multithreaded program that counts prime numbers within a large range, dividing the range among threads.

3. **Matrix Multiplication with Threads**: Implement multithreaded matrix multiplication, where each thread calculates a portion of the resulting matrix.

- **Multithreading**: Enables simultaneous execution of multiple tasks, improving efficiency on multicore systems.
- **Concurrency Control**: Mutexes prevent data races by ensuring only one thread accesses a shared resource at a time.
- **Thread Safety**: Proper synchronization, through mutexes or condition variables, is essential for safe concurrent programming.

Multithreading and concurrency are powerful techniques for building efficient, high-performance applications. By leveraging multiple threads and managing concurrency, you can create responsive, scalable programs that fully utilize modern hardware. In the next chapter, we'll explore networking in C++, covering socket programming and building simple client-server applications

CHAPTER 19: GUI PROGRAMMING WITH C++

Objective

This chapter provides a brief introduction to GUI (Graphical User Interface) programming in C++, covering popular libraries like Qt and SFML that make GUI development more accessible. We'll explore the basic concepts of GUI elements such as buttons, labels, and input fields, and create a simple calculator application as an example.

What is GUI Programming?

GUI programming allows developers to create applications with graphical interfaces, making them more interactive and user-friendly. Instead of relying solely on text-based input and output, GUI applications use windows, buttons, text fields, and other visual elements to improve usability.

Popular GUI Libraries in C++

1. **Qt**: A powerful, cross-platform framework for building complex GUI applications. Qt supports many platforms and includes features like drag-and-drop design, event handling, and a variety of GUI components.

2. **SFML (Simple and Fast Multimedia Library)**: A library primarily used for multimedia applications and 2D games but can be used for basic GUI applications. SFML is simpler

than Qt and provides quick access to windowing, graphics, and event handling.

For this chapter, we'll focus on **Qt**, as it's widely used in C++ GUI programming and provides extensive tools and documentation.

Setting Up Qt

1. **Download and Install Qt**:
   - Download the Qt installer from qt.io and follow the instructions to install it. Make sure to install the version that includes Qt Creator, the IDE specifically designed for Qt projects.
2. **Creating a Qt Project**:
   - Open Qt Creator, select *New Project*, choose *Application* > *Qt Widgets Application*, and follow the setup wizard to create a new GUI project.

Basic Components of a Qt GUI

1. **Main Window**: The main application window that holds all GUI elements.
2. **Widgets**: Basic GUI elements like buttons, labels, text boxes, and layout containers. Widgets are added to the main window to create the user interface.
3. **Signals and Slots**: A powerful event-handling mechanism in Qt, where *signals* (events) are emitted when something

happens, and *slots* (functions) handle those events. For example, clicking a button emits a signal that can trigger a slot function.

Example: Creating a Simple GUI Calculator

Let's create a simple calculator that performs basic arithmetic operations (addition, subtraction, multiplication, and division) using Qt.

1. **Setting Up the Project**
   - Create a new Qt Widgets Application project named CalculatorApp.

2. **Designing the GUI Layout**

   Open the MainWindow.ui file in Qt Creator's *Design* view and use drag-and-drop to design the calculator interface.

   - **Widgets**:
     - QLineEdit for the input field to display numbers and results.
     - QPushButton for the numbers 0-9 and arithmetic operations (+, -, *, /).
     - QPushButton for an = button to calculate the result and a C button to clear the display.
   - **Layout**:

- Arrange the number buttons in a grid layout and the operations on the side. Add the = and C buttons below the grid.

3. **Connecting Signals and Slots**

In Qt Creator, connect each button's clicked() signal to corresponding slot functions in the MainWindow class. Right-click on each button, select *Slot* from the context menu, and choose the clicked() signal to auto-generate the slot.

4. **Implementing the Calculator Logic**

Add the following code to mainwindow.cpp:

```cpp
#include "mainwindow.h"
#include "ui_mainwindow.h"
#include <QPushButton>
#include <QStack>

MainWindow::MainWindow(QWidget *parent) :
    QMainWindow(parent),
    ui(new Ui::MainWindow),
    pendingOperation(' '), operand1(0.0), operand2(0.0)
{
    ui->setupUi(this);
```

```
// Connect number buttons to a single slot
connect(ui->button0,    &QPushButton::clicked,    this,
&MainWindow::onDigitPressed);
    connect(ui->button1,    &QPushButton::clicked,    this,
&MainWindow::onDigitPressed);
    // Repeat for all buttons 2-9


    // Connect operation buttons
    connect(ui->buttonAdd,    &QPushButton::clicked,    this,
&MainWindow::onOperationPressed);
    connect(ui->buttonSubtract,    &QPushButton::clicked,
this, &MainWindow::onOperationPressed);
    connect(ui->buttonMultiply,    &QPushButton::clicked,
this, &MainWindow::onOperationPressed);
    connect(ui->buttonDivide, &QPushButton::clicked, this,
&MainWindow::onOperationPressed);


    // Connect equals and clear buttons
    connect(ui->buttonEquals, &QPushButton::clicked, this,
&MainWindow::onEqualsPressed);
    connect(ui->buttonClear, &QPushButton::clicked, this,
&MainWindow::onClearPressed);
}
```

```cpp
MainWindow::~MainWindow() {
    delete ui;
}

// Slot for digit buttons
void MainWindow::onDigitPressed() {
    QPushButton *button = qobject_cast<QPushButton*>(sender());
    QString buttonValue = button->text();
    ui->display->setText(ui->display->text() + buttonValue);
}

// Slot for operation buttons (+, -, *, /)
void MainWindow::onOperationPressed() {
    QPushButton *button = qobject_cast<QPushButton*>(sender());
    operand1 = ui->display->text().toDouble();
    pendingOperation = button->text().at(0).toLatin1();
    ui->display->clear();
}

// Slot for equals button
void MainWindow::onEqualsPressed() {
    operand2 = ui->display->text().toDouble();
    double result = 0.0;
```

```
switch (pendingOperation) {
    case '+': result = operand1 + operand2; break;
    case '-': result = operand1 - operand2; break;
    case '*': result = operand1 * operand2; break;
    case '/':
        if (operand2 != 0.0) result = operand1 / operand2;
        else ui->display->setText("Error");
        return;
}

ui->display->setText(QString::number(result));
operand1 = result; // Store result as operand1 for further
calculations
}

// Slot for clear button
void MainWindow::onClearPressed() {
    ui->display->clear();
    operand1 = operand2 = 0.0;
    pendingOperation = ' ';
}
```

5. **Explanation**

o **Digit Buttons**: The onDigitPressed slot appends the clicked button's digit to the display.

o **Operation Buttons**: The onOperationPressed slot stores the current display value as operand1, clears the display, and sets the pending operation (+, -, *, /).

o **Equals Button**: The onEqualsPressed slot reads the second operand from the display, performs the operation based on pendingOperation, and shows the result.

o **Clear Button**: The onClearPressed slot resets the calculator, clearing the display and resetting operands.

6. **Running the Calculator**

o Build and run the application in Qt Creator.

o Test the buttons to ensure that the calculator performs addition, subtraction, multiplication, division, and clears as expected.

Benefits of Using Qt for GUI Programming

1. **Cross-Platform Support**: Qt applications can be built for multiple platforms with minimal changes.

2. **Extensive Widgets and Features**: Qt provides a wide range of built-in widgets and tools, from simple buttons and labels to advanced tools like graphs and tables.

3. **Signal-Slot Mechanism**: Simplifies event handling, making it easy to link UI actions to functions.

4. **Rich Documentation and Community Support**: Qt is well-documented and has a large developer community, making it easy to find resources and troubleshoot issues.

Practice Exercises

1. **To-Do List Application**: Create a simple to-do list application with QLineEdit for input, a QPushButton to add tasks, and a QListWidget to display the tasks. Add functionality to mark tasks as completed.

2. **Temperature Converter**: Develop a temperature converter that takes a Celsius value and converts it to Fahrenheit and vice versa.

3. **Simple Text Editor**: Build a basic text editor with QTextEdit, QPushButton for saving and opening files, and QMenu for handling file operations.

- **GUI Programming**: Allows users to interact with applications visually using windows, buttons, and other graphical elements.

- **Qt Framework**: A powerful C++ library for building cross-platform GUI applications with a rich set of tools and widgets.

- **Signals and Slots**: A core feature in Qt for handling events, allowing for a clean and organized way to respond to user actions.

- **Event Handling and Widgets**: Essential for creating interactive applications that respond to user inputs, making GUI applications dynamic and user-friendly.

GUI programming with Qt is an effective way to create professional, interactive applications in C++. By mastering basic widgets, layout management, and event handling, you can build user-friendly programs that are both functional and visually appealing. In the next chapter, we'll explore networking in C++, covering the basics of socket programming and building simple client-server applications for data exchange.

CHAPTER 20: PROJECT – BUILDING A CONSOLE APPLICATION FROM SCRATCH

Objective

In this final chapter, we'll bring together all the concepts we've learned by building a console-based project: a *Personal Finance Manager*. This application will handle income and expenses, store data for persistence, and allow users to track their financial history. Through this project, readers will practice file handling, data structures, input validation, and program design.

Project Overview: Personal Finance Manager

The *Personal Finance Manager* will enable users to:

1. **Record Transactions**: Add entries for income and expenses with a description, amount, and date.

2. **View Financial Summary**: Display total income, total expenses, and the current balance.

3. **View Transaction History**: Display a list of all recorded transactions.

4. **Save and Load Data**: Store data in a file to maintain persistence across sessions.

Designing the Application

1. **Data Structure**

o Define a `Transaction` structure to hold details of each transaction.

o Use a `vector` to store all transactions.

2. **Menu Options**

o **Add Transaction**: Record income or expense.

o **View Summary**: Display total income, total expenses, and balance.

o **View All Transactions**: List all transactions with details.

o **Save Data**: Save transactions to a file.

o **Load Data**: Load transactions from a file at startup.

3. **File Handling**

o Use file I/O to read from and write to a data file, ensuring data persistence between sessions.

Implementation

1. **Define the Transaction Structure**

```cpp
Copy code
#include <string>

struct Transaction {
    std::string type;   // "Income" or "Expense"
    std::string description;
    double amount;
    std::string date;   // Date in "YYYY-MM-DD"
format
};
```

2. Define Functions for Menu Options

```cpp
Copy code
#include <iostream>
#include <vector>
#include <fstream>
#include <iomanip>

// Function declarations
void addTransaction(std::vector<Transaction>&
transactions);
void viewSummary(const
std::vector<Transaction>& transactions);
void viewAllTransactions(const
std::vector<Transaction>& transactions);
void saveData(const std::vector<Transaction>&
transactions, const std::string& filename);
void loadData(std::vector<Transaction>&
transactions, const std::string& filename);
```

3. Implement Main Menu and Input Handling

```cpp
Copy code
int main() {
    std::vector<Transaction> transactions;
    const std::string filename =
"finance_data.txt";

    // Load data from file at startup
    loadData(transactions, filename);

    int choice;
    do {
        std::cout << "\nPersonal Finance
Manager\n";
        std::cout << "1. Add Transaction\n";
        std::cout << "2. View Summary\n";
        std::cout << "3. View All
Transactions\n";
        std::cout << "4. Save Data\n";
        std::cout << "5. Exit\n";
        std::cout << "Enter your choice: ";
        std::cin >> choice;
```

```
switch (choice) {
    case 1:
        addTransaction(transactions);
        break;
    case 2:
        viewSummary(transactions);
        break;
    case 3:

viewAllTransactions(transactions);
        break;
    case 4:
        saveData(transactions,
filename);
        std::cout << "Data saved
successfully.\n";
        break;
    case 5:
        saveData(transactions,
filename); // Save data on exit
        std::cout << "Goodbye!\n";
        break;
    default:
        std::cout << "Invalid choice.
Please try again.\n";
    }
} while (choice != 5);

return 0;
}
```

4. **Function Implementations**
   o **Add Transaction**

```cpp
Copy code
void
addTransaction(std::vector<Transaction>&
transactions) {
    Transaction transaction;
    std::cout << "Enter type
(Income/Expense): ";
    std::cin >> transaction.type;
    std::cout << "Enter description: ";
```

```cpp
    std::cin.ignore();
    std::getline(std::cin,
transaction.description);
    std::cout << "Enter amount: ";
    std::cin >> transaction.amount;
    std::cout << "Enter date (YYYY-MM-
DD): ";
    std::cin >> transaction.date;

    transactions.push_back(transaction);
    std::cout << "Transaction added
successfully.\n";
}
```

o **View Summary**

cpp
Copy code
```cpp
void viewSummary(const
std::vector<Transaction>& transactions) {
    double totalIncome = 0.0;
    double totalExpenses = 0.0;

    for (const auto& transaction :
transactions) {
        if (transaction.type == "Income")
{
            totalIncome +=
transaction.amount;
        } else if (transaction.type ==
"Expense") {
            totalExpenses +=
transaction.amount;
        }
    }

    double balance = totalIncome -
totalExpenses;
    std::cout << std::fixed <<
std::setprecision(2);
    std::cout << "Total Income: $" <<
totalIncome << "\n";
    std::cout << "Total Expenses: $" <<
totalExpenses << "\n";
```

```cpp
    std::cout << "Balance: $" << balance
<< "\n";
}
```

o **View All Transactions**

```cpp
cpp
Copy code
void viewAllTransactions(const
std::vector<Transaction>& transactions) {
    std::cout << "\nTransaction
History:\n";
    for (const auto& transaction :
transactions) {
        std::cout << transaction.date <<
" | " << transaction.type
                 << " | " <<
transaction.description << " | $"
                 << std::fixed <<
std::setprecision(2) <<
transaction.amount << "\n";
    }
}
```

o **Save Data to File**

```cpp
cpp
Copy code
void saveData(const
std::vector<Transaction>& transactions,
const std::string& filename) {
    std::ofstream file(filename);
    if (file.is_open()) {
        for (const auto& transaction :
transactions) {
            file << transaction.type <<
","
                 <<
transaction.description << ","
                 << transaction.amount <<
","
                 << transaction.date <<
"\n";
        }
```

```
        file.close();
    } else {
        std::cout << "Unable to open file
for saving.\n";
    }
}
```

o **Load Data from File**

```cpp
Copy code
void loadData(std::vector<Transaction>&
transactions, const std::string&
filename) {
    std::ifstream file(filename);
    if (file.is_open()) {
        transactions.clear();
        Transaction transaction;
        std::string amountStr;

        while (getline(file,
transaction.type, ',') &&
                getline(file,
transaction.description, ',') &&
                getline(file, amountStr,
',') &&
                getline(file,
transaction.date)) {
            transaction.amount =
std::stod(amountStr);

transactions.push_back(transaction);
        }
        file.close();
    } else {
        std::cout << "No saved data
found. Starting fresh.\n";
    }
}
```

Explanation of the Code

1. **Transaction Structure**: Holds the details of each transaction, including the type, description, amount, and date.

2. **Main Menu**: Provides options to add, view, and save transactions, along with a summary.

3. **File I/O**:

   o saveData: Saves the transaction vector to a file, with each transaction on a new line in a comma-separated format.

   o loadData: Reads from the file and populates the transactions vector on startup.

4. **Input Validation**: Basic validation is handled in the main menu, allowing for controlled inputs. More comprehensive validation (e.g., date format checking) can be added for further robustness.

Sample Output

```mathematica
Copy code
Personal Finance Manager
1. Add Transaction
2. View Summary
3. View All Transactions
4. Save Data
5. Exit
Enter your choice: 1
Enter type (Income/Expense): Income
Enter description: Salary
Enter amount: 1500
Enter date (YYYY-MM-DD): 2024-05-01
Transaction added successfully.

Personal Finance Manager
1. Add Transaction
```

```
2. View Summary
3. View All Transactions
4. Save Data
5. Exit
Enter your choice: 2
Total Income: $1500.00
Total Expenses: $0.00
Balance: $1500.00
```

Summary of the Concepts Used

- **Structures**: Used to define Transaction for easy data management.
- **Vectors**: Used to store a dynamic list of transactions.
- **Functions**: Modularized code for adding transactions, viewing summaries, and file I/O.
- **File Handling**: Provides data persistence by saving and loading transactions from a file.
- **User Input and Validation**: Basic user input handling ensures smooth program flow.

Practice and Expansion Ideas

1. **Advanced Date Handling**: Validate and format dates properly, and allow transactions to be filtered by date.
2. **Category Tags**: Add a category field to transactions, allowing users to track expenses by category (e.g., food, rent, entertainment).
3. **Monthly Reports**: Implement monthly or yearly summaries, showing income and expenses over time.

4. **Encryption**: Add encryption to the saved file for added privacy in personal finance data.

- **Console Application Development**: Building a functional application by combining multiple C++ concepts.
- **File Persistence**: Saving and loading data allows the application to retain information across sessions.
- **Modular Design**: Breaking down the program into functions simplifies maintenance and scalability.
- **Input Validation**: Ensures users enter data in expected formats, making the program more robust.

This project serves as a practical example of applying C++ concepts in a real-world application, providing hands-on experience with program structure, data handling, and user interaction. Congratulations on completing this project and your journey through C++ programming fundamentals and advanced concepts!

CHAPTER 21: NETWORKING IN JAVA

Networking in Java allows applications to communicate over the internet or local networks. Java's java.net package provides classes for creating networked applications that can send and receive data using TCP/IP protocols. This chapter introduces you to Java's networking capabilities, covering sockets, client-server models, and URL handling. By the end of this chapter, you'll understand how to create networked applications that can exchange data, handle multiple clients, and retrieve information from the web.

21.1 Introduction to Networking Concepts

Networking enables computers and applications to communicate with each other, facilitating data exchange and collaboration over the internet or local networks. Common networking protocols include:

1. **TCP (Transmission Control Protocol)**: A connection-oriented protocol ensuring reliable data transfer.
2. **UDP (User Datagram Protocol)**: A connectionless protocol that allows faster, but less reliable, data transfer.

Java's networking classes primarily focus on TCP and UDP protocols to build applications that can transfer data over a network.

21.2 IP Addresses and Ports

Every device connected to a network has a unique **IP address**. A **port** is a logical endpoint used to identify a specific application or process on a device. When setting up network communication, both the IP address and port number are required to target a specific service on a networked device.

Example of an IP Address and Port

- IP Address: 192.168.1.100
- Port: 8080

A web server may use IP address 192.168.1.100 and port 8080 to communicate with clients.

21.3 The Socket Class

The **Socket** class represents a client socket, which is an endpoint for communication between two machines. A client socket is used to connect to a server and exchange data.

Creating a Client Socket

java

Copy code

```
import java.io.*;
import java.net.Socket;

public class ClientExample {
    public static void main(String[] args) {
```

```
try (Socket socket = new Socket("localhost", 8080);
    PrintWriter out = new
PrintWriter(socket.getOutputStream(), true);
    BufferedReader in = new BufferedReader(new
InputStreamReader(socket.getInputStream()))) {

    out.println("Hello, Server!");
    String response = in.readLine();
    System.out.println("Server says: " + response);

} catch (IOException e) {
    e.printStackTrace();
}
}
}
```

In this example:

- Socket connects to a server on localhost at port 8080.
- PrintWriter and BufferedReader are used to send and receive messages.

21.4 The ServerSocket Class

The **ServerSocket** class represents a server socket that waits for client connections on a specific port. The server socket listens for incoming connections and, once a connection is established, interacts with the client through an individual Socket instance.

Creating a Server Socket

java

Copy code

```java
import java.io.*;
import java.net.ServerSocket;
import java.net.Socket;

public class ServerExample {
    public static void main(String[] args) {
        try (ServerSocket serverSocket = new ServerSocket(8080)) {
            System.out.println("Server is listening on port 8080...");

            while (true) {
                Socket clientSocket = serverSocket.accept();
                System.out.println("Client connected");

                PrintWriter                out              =              new
PrintWriter(clientSocket.getOutputStream(), true);
                BufferedReader   in   =   new   BufferedReader(new
InputStreamReader(clientSocket.getInputStream()));

                String message = in.readLine();
                System.out.println("Received from client: " + message);

                out.println("Hello, Client!");
```

```
        clientSocket.close();

      }


    } catch (IOException e) {

      e.printStackTrace();

    }

  }

}
```

In this example:

- ServerSocket listens on port 8080.
- When a client connects, accept() returns a Socket for communication.
- The server responds with "Hello, Client!" and closes the connection.

21.5 Client-Server Communication Model

In the client-server model:

1. The **client** initiates communication, sending requests to the server.
2. The **server** responds to client requests, typically listening on a specific port.

A **simple chat application** or **web server** can be built using this model, with clients sending messages to the server and the server processing and responding to them.

21.6 Handling Multiple Clients with Multithreading

To handle multiple clients simultaneously, the server can create a new thread for each client connection. This allows the server to interact with multiple clients concurrently without blocking other connections.

Example: Multithreaded Server

1. **Define the ClientHandler Class**:

```java
Copy code
import java.io.*;
import java.net.Socket;

public class ClientHandler extends Thread {
    private Socket clientSocket;

    public ClientHandler(Socket socket) {
        this.clientSocket = socket;
    }

    @Override
```

```java
public void run() {
    try      (PrintWriter      out      =      new
PrintWriter(clientSocket.getOutputStream(), true);
        BufferedReader  in  =  new  BufferedReader(new
InputStreamReader(clientSocket.getInputStream())))  {

        String message = in.readLine();
        System.out.println("Received  from  client:  "  +
message);
        out.println("Hello, Client!");

    } catch (IOException e) {
        e.printStackTrace();
    }
  }
}
```

2. **Update the Server to Use ClientHandler**:

```java
java
Copy code
import java.net.ServerSocket;
import java.net.Socket;

public class MultithreadedServer {
    public static void main(String[] args) {
```

```
try (ServerSocket serverSocket = new
ServerSocket(8080)) {
    System.out.println("Server is listening on port
8080...");

        while (true) {
            Socket clientSocket = serverSocket.accept();
            System.out.println("New client connected");

            ClientHandler handler = new
ClientHandler(clientSocket);
            handler.start();
        }

    } catch (IOException e) {
        e.printStackTrace();
    }
  }
}
```

In this example:

- Each client connection is handled by a separate ClientHandler thread, allowing concurrent connections.

21.7 DatagramSocket for UDP Communication

For connectionless communication, Java provides DatagramSocket and DatagramPacket for sending and receiving data using the **UDP** protocol. UDP is faster than TCP but does not guarantee reliable data delivery.

Example: UDP Server and Client

1. **Define the UDP Server**:

```java
Copy code
import java.net.DatagramPacket;
import java.net.DatagramSocket;

public class UDPServer {
    public static void main(String[] args) {
        try (DatagramSocket serverSocket = new DatagramSocket(8080)) {
            byte[] buffer = new byte[256];
            DatagramPacket packet = new DatagramPacket(buffer, buffer.length);

            System.out.println("UDP Server is listening on port 8080...");

            while (true) {
```

```java
            serverSocket.receive(packet);
            String message = new String(packet.getData(), 0,
packet.getLength());
            System.out.println("Received: " + message);
          }

      } catch (Exception e) {
        e.printStackTrace();
      }
    }
}
```

2. **Define the UDP Client**:

java
Copy code

```java
import java.net.DatagramPacket;
import java.net.DatagramSocket;
import java.net.InetAddress;

public class UDPClient {
    public static void main(String[] args) {
        try (DatagramSocket socket = new DatagramSocket())
{
            String message = "Hello, UDP Server!";
            byte[] buffer = message.getBytes();
```

```java
        InetAddress          address          =
InetAddress.getByName("localhost");


        DatagramPacket        packet      =        new
DatagramPacket(buffer, buffer.length, address, 8080);
        socket.send(packet);


    } catch (Exception e) {
        e.printStackTrace();
    }
  }
}
```

In this example:

- The UDP server listens on port 8080 and receives packets.
- The UDP client sends a packet containing "Hello, UDP Server!" to the server.

21.8 Using URL and URLConnection for HTTP Requests

Java provides the URL and URLConnection classes for making HTTP requests, enabling applications to retrieve data from web servers.

Example: Fetching Data from a URL

java

Copy code

```java
import java.io.BufferedReader;
import java.io.InputStreamReader;
import java.net.URL;

public class URLExample {
    public static void main(String[] args) {
        try {
            URL                url                =                new
URL("https://jsonplaceholder.typicode.com/posts/1");
            BufferedReader    in    =    new    BufferedReader(new
InputStreamReader(url.openStream()));

            String line;
            while ((line = in.readLine()) != null) {
                System.out.println(line);
            }

            in.close();

        } catch (Exception e) {
            e.printStackTrace();
        }
    }
}
```

In this example:

- URL connects to a JSON placeholder API endpoint.
- The content of the response is read line by line and printed to the console.

21.9 Practical Example: Simple Chat Server

Let's create a simple chat server that allows multiple clients to send messages to each other using the TCP protocol.

1. **Define the ChatClientHandler Class**:

```java
Copy code
import java.io.*;
import java.net.Socket;

public class ChatClientHandler extends Thread {
    private Socket clientSocket;
    private PrintWriter out;

    public ChatClientHandler(Socket socket) {
        this.clientSocket = socket;
    }

    @Override
    public void run() {
```

```java
    try (BufferedReader in = new BufferedReader(new
InputStreamReader(clientSocket.getInputStream())))  {
        out                  =                  new
PrintWriter(clientSocket.getOutputStream(), true);

        String message;
        while ((message = in.readLine()) != null) {
            System.out.println("Message from client: " +
message);
            out.println("Server received: " + message);
        }

    } catch (IOException e) {
        e.printStackTrace();
    }
}

    public PrintWriter getOut() {
        return out;
    }
}
```

2. **Update the Server to Manage Multiple Clients**:

java
Copy code

```java
import java.net.ServerSocket;
import java.net.Socket;
import java.util.ArrayList;
import java.util.List;

public class ChatServer {
    private static List<ChatClientHandler> clients = new
ArrayList<>();

    public static void main(String[] args) {
        try     (ServerSocket      serverSocket     =     new
ServerSocket(8080)) {
            System.out.println("Chat server is running...");

            while (true) {
                Socket clientSocket = serverSocket.accept();
                ChatClientHandler     clientHandler     =     new
ChatClientHandler(clientSocket);
                clients.add(clientHandler);
                clientHandler.start();
            }

        } catch (IOException e) {
            e.printStackTrace();
        }
```

```
        }

    }
```

In this example:

- ChatClientHandler manages individual client connections.
- ChatServer listens for clients and creates a new ChatClientHandler thread for each client.

21.10 Best Practices for Networking

1. **Use Multithreading**: Use separate threads to handle multiple clients or long-running requests.
2. **Close Resources**: Ensure sockets, input/output streams, and other resources are closed after use.
3. **Handle Exceptions Gracefully**: Network code is susceptible to exceptions; ensure proper handling.
4. **Use Timeouts**: Set timeouts on sockets to prevent indefinite waiting.
5. **Secure Network Communication**: Encrypt sensitive data and use secure protocols (like HTTPS) when necessary.

21.11 Practice Exercises

1. **Echo Server**:
   o Create a server that echoes messages sent by the client. Allow multiple clients to connect simultaneously.

2. **File Transfer Application**:

   o Build a client-server application to transfer files from one machine to another using sockets.

3. **Chat Room with UDP**:

   o Create a chat application using DatagramSocket and UDP packets. Allow multiple users to send and receive messages.

4. **Web Scraper**:

   o Write a program that uses URL and URLConnection to fetch and parse data from a website.

5. **Simple HTTP Server**:

   o Create a basic HTTP server using ServerSocket that can serve HTML files to a web browser.

21.12 Summary

In this chapter, we explored Java's networking capabilities, covering sockets, client-server models, and URL handling. You learned how to create TCP and UDP servers and clients, handle multiple client connections, and retrieve web content using HTTP. Networking in Java enables applications to communicate over local and wide-area networks, making it a fundamental skill for building distributed applications.

In the next chapter, we'll cover **Java Database Connectivity (JDBC)**, allowing applications to interact with databases for data storage, retrieval, and manipulation, a key aspect of many enterprise applications.

www.ingramcontent.com/pod-product-compliance
Lightning Source LLC
Chambersburg PA
CBHW071242050326
40690CB00011B/2225